99 STRATEGIES
TO GET CUSTOMERS

You may have 99 problems, but getting
your next customer won't be one!

Flavilla Fongang

For my mother, Julienne Ngassa, who taught me how to be wise and free.

Acknowledgements

Writing this book was a fantastic moment that I wish everyone to experience. After finishing it, I felt new, fulfilled, and like a gift from God to you. I'm already writing another book. These are lies! I wanted to die every day but knowing you are smiling or even laughing reading these words makes it all worth it. So, I'm glad I didn't give up.

I would like to thank my amazing design team and marketing team at 3 Colours Rule for supporting me in creating this book for you: Chinyere Okoroafo, Avni Lalji, Yasin Yousef, Zahra Siddiqui and Ogechi Joseph.

To my family and friends, thanks for your endless support.

Finally, I would like to thank you for choosing my book. I hope this book helps you achieve all your dreams.

TABLE OF CONTENTS

INTRODUCTION:

Read this FIRST before diving in

As you are reading this book, know that I'm smiling, because I know at least one of these 99 strategies will help you thrive. I wrote this book as the United Kingdom was entering a recession as a result of COVID19. Many businesses have been negatively affected by COVID 19. 2020 will remain a year we wish we could forget, except for Zoom, Amazon, Netflix, and Disney. In situations like this, businesses and entrepreneurs would be well advised to work with a creative agency like my own, 3 Colours Rule, to help them strategically re-evaluate their marketing and sales activities. The dilemma, in most cases, is that companies have financial limitations. So, to support small businesses, marketers, and entrepreneurs unable to work with an agency, I launched my online branding and marketing programme to help them build their brand resilience. Naturally, on the back of that, I wrote this book as the perfect addition.

Many companies have failed, not because of the quality of their services and/or products, but because they aren't effectively articulating their unique set of values and consequently struggle to attract prospects to convert into customers. So, here you will discover 99 strategies that will get you closer to your next customers. Before you jump in, I have made an assumption about you. Yes, I have. For these 99 strategies to work effectively, I have assumed that you have a great brand. If that is the case, this book will become your business bible. If you aren't sure if you have a great brand, follow the system I created, the D.A.C. system. Most businesses fail because they do not effectively apply the D.A.C. system.

In the D.A.C. system, D stands for Distinguish. This is phase 1, where you develop a strong brand strategy so you can articulate a relevant and unique value proposition that resonates with your specific target audience.

In the D.A.C. system, A stands for Attract. This is phase 2, where you have chosen your brand positioning, your target audience and how to stand out, and now need to make your brand visual presentation align with these options. If you decided your brand strategy was to target wealthy individuals, your brand identity should suit to attract them. So, choosing your tone of voice, colours, fonts, imagery, brand associations, and more are crucial.

In the D.A.C. system, C stands for Convert. This is phase 3. Now you have a distinguishable and attractive brand; you can focus on reaching prospects, partners, media etc. to drive business. This is where this book will help you. Now you understand why I mentioned earlier that I had made an assumption.

If you need guidance on how to successfully work on phases 1 & 2 of the D.A.C. system, I have created a complimentary online brand growth programme that you can access right now by visiting www.coaching.flavillafongang.com I have also added at the end of the book my D.A.C. system - The 90-day action plan.

Don't say I don't love you.

I hope you find excitement in learning all the things I have absorbed over the years and that I am sharing with you. The only thing I ask in return is to share with me how the book has helped you.

OK! Are you ready to dive in? Make sure you have your notepad as I have written this content to stimulate your brain, and loads of ideas will come to you. Write them down and review them all when you have read the entire book.

IMPORTANT!

Some of the strategies I am going to share with you will feel familiar, but please don't skip anything as you might discover new ways to apply them. I will reveal how to do them right if they didn't work for you in the past, or if you have never tried them.

At the end of the book, I have added further explanations with regards to the marketing and sales terminology used throughout the book.

With all my heart

Flavilla Fongang

HOW SHOULD YOU READ THIS BOOK?

I advise you to read it twice! Why? Because there is a great deal of information to absorb, and I want to make sure you don't miss anything significant to you.

Have a notepad handy. Ideas will flow through your mind, so be ready to write them down, but don't take action until you finish reading the entire book.

At the end, apply my 'end in mind' customer acquisition plan.

Take action immediately. You invested money in getting this book, so make it work for you.

At the end of each strategy, I indicate the price, complexity, and time required to put that strategy in place. This will help you develop your marketing and sales plan.

Budget: ££££

Complexity: Hire an expert

Time required: A few days

SECTION 1:

The right setup to maximise conversion

Strategy 1 – Sales skills and CRM

This is, by far, the most important strategy. If neither you nor anyone in your business knows how to sell your services or products effectively, you will struggle to thrive and scale-up. Most people start a business because they are great at what they do or passionate about changing the world, but they have no sales skills. They end up commoditising their bespoke offerings, offering discounts, or working with clients they don't really like. This consequently impacts on their margins and work-life balance, and they feel emotionally deflated.

Selling is a skill, and the sooner you learn how to sell, the more prospects will convert into customers. My first advice is to get properly trained, or hire a sales consultant, or leverage an employee with a great track record of successfully selling what you offer. Remember, you still need to generate leads for them to convert. Lead generation and prospect conversion are two sets of skills. The below strategies will reveal how to do that.

My second most significant advice is that selling is not enough without customer relationship management or CRM. It's impossible to remember all the people you spoke to last week unless you have the memory of an elephant. Having a CRM in place to support your sales activities will ensure you are always reaching out to your prospects and customers the right way and at the right time.

How to use a CRM effectively to convert more prospects into customers:

- Record details of every sale interaction with a prospect, so when you reconnect with them, you remember where you left off.
- Always end every conversation with an agreement with regards to the next step, so they are expecting you to reach out at an agreed time. Note this in your CRM so you can get an email reminder.
- Get in the habit of communicating with your prospect regularly in order to build credibility and/or to convert into customers.

Some sales cycles can be as long as three months to two years, so patience and consistency are essential.

- With CRM in place, you can easily handover sales leads to another person because the information isn't kept in your head.

- If you do business with the intention to help, it is your responsibility to pre-empt the next solutions your clients will require to support their goals. For example, if a customer buys a car, you should add to your CRM when the next MOT is due and contact them accordingly. When the customer is on-site, evaluate if there are any additional needs that can be fulfilled. Use your CRM to identify when it is time to upsell additional services to your existing clients.

The sooner you integrate a CRM, the better it will be to keep your data accurate.

Budget: From 0 to ££££ - This varies according to the software you choose, data you own, and features you may require

Complexity: Easy

Time required: Immediate implementation

Strategy 2 – A website that converts

This may also seem so obvious that you may wonder why I chose to include it. Creating a website for your brand is one of the most effective ways to attract new customers, but guess what? 30% of businesses still don't have a website. Having a website is not an outdated strategy, as today's consumers believe companies with a professional website are more credible than those that don't have one. Why? Because business is like love. A website is part of the first stage of relationship building; it's the first encounter. Let them get to know you and explore the discovery. Remember, don't move too slowly, but don't move too fast. Have the right marketing strategies in place, so you don't lose touch and can move to the next phase of your sales funnel.

Your website is the shop window for your business. Having a bad website is as bad as not having a website. Before you start spending millions of pounds on developing a new website, having a clear website strategy from the start will allow you to quickly make a fast return on investment.

Here are three top questions you need to answer:

1. **Purpose - What is the purpose of your website?**

Is the intention to present your work, sell online, generate leads, or something else? The clarity of understanding the purpose of your website from the start will help you create the right website structure strategy. See your website as a funnel and create a journey that leads you to the goals you desire to achieve. Take into consideration the best way to communicate with your prospects or customers by considering adding a telephone number, Chatbox, 'Contact us' form, or even a demonstration booking option.

2. **User experience - What type of user experience do you need to create for your website visitors?**

Focus on usability and user experience (UX). As yourself, "How will my visitors be more likely to visit my website? On their phone or desktop?" Your communication strategy (social media, email, advertising, etc..) will help you figure out what you should focus on first. If you already have a website, check out the analytics to figure out the most popular device format. If your audience is B2B, focus on your desktop experience. If your audience is B2C, focus on your mobile experience.

3. **Value proposition - Why is your company different from the competition?**

Without having to scroll down, your potential customers should be able to grasp your niche, your uniqueness, and your value. This should be articulated simply in one sentence. Lemlist, a company specialising in helping companies send cold emails to prospects, has a very clear value proposition: "Send cold emails that get replies." Love it! It's short, clear, and to the point. If you are familiar with my neuromarketing work, I talk a lot about the importance of using stimuli such as customer testimonials, case studies, stories, reviews from third-party consumer websites, and visuals. So, think about those as well.

4. **Evolve**

Your website will evolve. Always develop a fully editable website. I have been in business for more than ten years, and my first website looked nothing like the one I have now. To evolve, listen and learn continuously from your customers, your prospects, your team, and anyone with constructive feedback.

Budget: From £ to ££££ - This varies according to your business and web requirements

Complexity: Easy to complex

Time required: Days to months

Strategy 3 – A landing page

Now, you're probably thinking, "Why do I need a landing page when I have a website. Is it not enough, Flavilla?" Website is different from a landing page. A landing page is a targeted page, used to convert as many visitors into leads as possible. A landing page doesn't have any title headers, such as home, contact us, etc., that you typically see at the top of a website. A landing page is one page.

Your landing page is part of your marketing campaign. If you are ready to promote a product or service or build your mailing list, you need a landing page. A landing page prevents all sorts of distractions a visitor may encounter when visiting your website. A website has various calls to actions, such as a contact us button, view more button, see our testimonials etc. On the other hand, a landing page only has one call to action: download this book, book a call, or grab this offer.

A landing page copy is designed for one specific niche and written like a sales letter. So, if you have various target audiences, you should design different landing pages for different prospects. The more you use words that resonate with each of your target audiences, the better you will be able to convert.

If you are familiar with my neuromarketing work, I explain in detail in my online branding and marketing programme the importance of using different stimuli to engage prospects.

To create a successful landing page, consider the following:

1. **Set your intention and define your audience**

   What is the goal of this landing page and who do you want to target? Pick a niche: Choosing hairdressers is better than targeting beauty brands as it is too broad. Before promoting your landing page, make sure you have clearly thought about the entire sales funnel process, from a visitor leaving their email address to them becoming a customer.

2. Create a catchy, surprising, and desirable headline

Here is an example: "Discover how to lose 5 kilos in 2 weeks without having to exercise. Get this free ebook." You can have an optional sub-headline, for example, "Discover the health secrets celebrities use to always look great on the red carpet." This sentence says it all, and I bet you would want this book if it existed.

3. A brief description

Your title should be followed by a description of your offer and the benefits it brings if your visitors take the offer.

4. Use visuals

An image is worth a thousand words, so use a photo or a video to compliment your short description and client success stories.

5. Talk less, show more

This is where you can add some credibility to your offer supporting proof elements such as video or written testimonials with photos, customer logos, or security badges. If you intend to sell directly on your landing page, adding a money-back guarantee makes your offer more appealing and risk-free.

6. A clear call to action

Now you have done all this work convincing them to believe in your brand, use a form to capture information.

Remember, we are naturally risk-averse; your copy needs to reinforce your credibility, reassure that you are a safe choice to make, speak to their desire or pain, and drive them to act immediately, not tomorrow.

Budget: £

Complexity: Easy

Time required: A day or two

Strategy 4 – Ecommerce social media

If social media is a dominant part of your marketing strategy and/or if you have large and active followings, you should use social media to sell your products and/or services directly. Ecommerce social media is the use of social media platforms to market directly to an eCommerce store. Your eCommerce is integrated within your social media pages. If you have a strong social media presence with engaged followers, you should actively utilise your social pages to generate online sales.

How to do it right?

- If you are selling a single product, such as an ebook, integrate a direct link on your profile pages.

- Optimise your website for search engines; if they can't find you, they can't buy from you.

- Integrate your social media accounts to your website so your post can be linked to a specific eCommerce page.

- Optimise to run PPC campaigns to reach users while they are searching for products similar to yours.

- Use social media to communicate in a less formal way with potential customers. Make it easy for them to engage with your brand and learn more about your products.

Budget: 0

Complexity: Easy

Time required: Continuously

Strategy 5 - Business cards

If you know me, you'll know that I am the queen of networking. Yes, I love talking to strangers. OK, I sound crazy. Business cards have become an integrated part of networking etiquette. You talk with someone, and if you want to stay in touch, you exchange business cards. So, let me ask you this. How many other people's cards do you have, and do you remember the person who gave it to you? I'm guessing many, and you don't.

Business cards should be a way to express what you do. Let me explain. When I started networking, I wanted to stand out. So, I used to give plastic business cards, then I moved to glossy, square, black cards. It is sexy and memorable. It is a business card the receiver doesn't want to throw away. It is aligned with what I do and who I am. I am a brand strategist; I understand the art of distinction.

Instead of giving standard, boring business cards, be creative and make a statement that will make an impact on the receiver. Start thinking about your business cards as marketing tools and not just contact information that can be found on LinkedIn.

How to transform your business card into a customer acquisition tool:

- Choose unusual shapes and/or texture.
- Add a QR code that links to a company presentation.
- Add your face if you are pretty. I'm joking!
- Add testimonials to add credibility.
- Give a special offer to get them to reconnect with you soon.
- Add your value proposition statement to set your brand apart.

Budget: £

Complexity: Easy

Time required: Continuously

Strategy 6 – QR code

QR stands for Quick Response. Did you know that? When the code is scanned with a smartphone, it provides information from a transitory media. QR codes have increased in popularity and won't stop with digital proliferation.

The reason why QR codes are effective is that they can store a large amount of data such as URL links, geo coordinates, and text. This means you are no longer obliged to print marketing materials. All smartphones can scan QR codes, and you can easily generate a QR code without needing the help of a QR code developer. Add a QR code to your business cards so you can keep it simple and tease curiosity, which will engage the receiver to scan the QR code in order to discover what it reveals.

What you can use QR codes for:

- Brochure
- Videos
- Product
- Contact
- Offer
- Event
- Competition
- Coupon
- Social media

Budget: 0

Complexity: Easy

Time required: Few minutes

SECTION 2:

Getting discovered

Strategy 7 – Get discovered with SEO

What is the point of having a great brand that no one can find? Yes, it is completely useless. SEO is often overlooked because most people want results right now. But if you want your business to last and to generate regular leads, SEO should be part of your long-term business growth strategy. Plus, using Google AdWords can be very pricey, and most people have an ad blocker on their devices.

Here is the best way to describe successful SEO. It's about getting search engines to fall in love with your business. Google is the most used search engine, and its job is to provide its users with the best search results in a fraction of a second. Your job is to help Google do this job. You may ask, how do I do that, Flavi? I will give you some tips, but if your market is very saturated, I highly recommend working with an SEO consultant.

Understand your client's customer journey. Your business mindset should always be to want to help. It is your responsibility to provide as much useful and valuable information that will support your potential clients before they are even ready to buy from you. If you were a personal trainer, this is the kind of useful content you could create:

- How to eat healthy food that keeps you fuller for longer.
- How to choose the right training programme for my body goal.
- How to not gain weight over Christmas.
- How to lose weight for summer.

This is great, evergreen content. Evergreen content means this content will never be outdated and always relevant. To appear in the news, you can also create non-evergreen content to get attention to your brand. "How to get your booty looking like Kim Kardashian's without surgery." This content is non-evergreen as it is unlikely to be relevant in ten years. Many technologies, such as Yoast, allow you to do your own SEO. I have added at the end of the book my favourite tech tools.

1. **Google keywords**

Use Google keywords search to discover the keywords that are most searched by your prospects. Always choose highly targeted and popular keywords instead of broad ones. For example, Instead of targeting "London personal trainers" target "Personal trainers in Covent Garden." It might not have the same search volume, but the chance of your website ranking for this keyword is easier, quicker, and less competitive. You can start by picking six to eight keywords to always use in your content. One of my first businesses was my online fashion styling academy. I hired an SEO consultant at the start; then, when my team was more knowledgeable, we ran it internally. Now, for the last ten years, my website ranks on the first page of Google for my lead generation keywords.

2. Yoast plugin

This website plugin will help you optimise your page rankings and outsmart the competition. Basically, this plugin works as your SEO consultant who evaluates whether your website content meets the highest technical SEO standards. It also advises you on how to bring your content to the highest standards of SEO while improving your overall readability.

3. Use primary keywords in your title and page descriptions

Make sure to use your keywords as often as you can both in your page title and page descriptions so search engines can identify if your content is relevant to the searches being made. When you make a habit of adding your keywords through the content you create, search engines will identify your site's focus or niche and recommend you more and more.

4. Add a description for your images

Don't miss the opportunity to be discovered through image searches. Add the alt text for your images to describe them for search engines. When writing alt text for your website images, keep your description concise and related to the image. The temptation to insert your keywords is strong, but please don't as this could have a negative impact on SEO.

5. Use internal links on your website

Internal linking refers to any links from one page of your domain that is linked to another page within your same domain. Internally linking your content will support your SEO efforts and drive traffic to other pages. Imagine a visitor reading one of your pages; when they reach the end of the page, you should suggest other pages for them to read. Your internal linking should be aligned with your website strategy: mailing list building, a purchase, booking a demo, or something else.

6.   Speed up your page load time

Don't let the poor speed of your website take your visitors away. Make sure your website loads in seconds as visitors have a poor attention span. Having a slow website affects the number of visitors, decreasing your conversion rates and website search rank.

To reduce website load time, hire an SEO consultant to:

- Compress images and optimise files.
- Fix browser caching.
- Minimise HTTP requests.
- Utilise CDNs and remove unused scripts/files.

Budget: ££

Complexity: Get trained or hire an expert

Time required: Continuously

Strategy 8 – Online directories

Should you still bother with web directories? Yes! But why? You are probably thinking. If you are as old as I am, you will remember the days of five-kilo Yellow Pages directory books. You could find every business there. Loads of things have changed since then, but it doesn't mean online directories are no longer relevant.

Online directories are a source of traffic and trust. If you operate within a certain region, you definitely need to be in online directories to maintain your local citations. This will help you get the credibility and consequently will drive traffic to your website. This is also part of your web link building strategy.

When searching for online directories, keep those two criteria in mind:

- Only register on reputable online directories such as yell.com or Google My Business.
- Only register on online directories where your audience is likely to search for your service; for example, if you run Mini Cooper road trip events, register on Mini Cooper networks where your potential customers are.

Budget: 0

Complexity: Easy

Time required: Few hours

Strategy 9 – Get Googled

Google My Business is, of course, a must. Shockingly, a lot of businesses haven't registered their business on Google My Business and are missing out on many business opportunities. This free, local marketing tool is the equivalent of the yellow pages decades ago and allows businesses to list their business on Google Search and Google Maps.

Unlike other online directories, you should also:

- Allow visitors to ask questions and share your business information.
- Post daily posts and events on social media; the more active you are, the more Google will favour you.
- Invite your customers to review your business; when it comes to Google reviews, the goal is to get between 4.5 and 5 stars.

All of this will have a positive impact on driving traffic and sales. Spend some time to complete all the information and use all the features on Google, and it will pay off.

Budget: 0

Complexity: Easy

Time required: Few hours

Strategy 10 – Weblink building

Creating great content and linking internally is great, but it's not always enough to rank quickly enough on the first page of search engines. The word web sounds pretty self-explanatory. The more your website is connected to highly ranked websites, the more likely you are to rank and be found by your ideal prospects.

Here are the few strategies you can apply to link your website to strong websites:

- **Get featured in the news**

That's where media presence is important. If your website links with the BBC or any highly ranked website, your website gains authority. When you get featured in the news, ask them to add your website URL on their page. I know what you are thinking; it is easier said than done. I agree, but it is not impossible. It requires persistence and being recognised by journalists. That's where building your brand, or your personal brand is crucial.

- **Guest blog**

Become a guest blogger for respected media such as Forbes or a local online newspaper.

I suggest approaching those brands with great subjects relevant to the news. Suggest writing the article on their behalf for an exchange of a link to their website.

- **Directory listings**

Yellow pages might be a thing from the past, but online directory listings still exist. Getting listed on other websites' directories designed for your specific target will improve your website ranking and the chances of being discovered by potential customers. For example, if your target audience is mums, you should definitely list your website on Mumsnet, and other website directories created for mums.

Budget: 0

Complexity: Easy to moderate

Time required: Continuously

Strategy 11 – Guest blogging

Guest blogging remains one of the best inbound marketing strategies, but unfortunately, it is rarely used enough or very well. Use guest blogging to share your expertise and present your business on another company's website.

Through defining your prospect persona, you would have identified their interests and other brands they like. Your goal is to guest blog on websites that attract your prospects. If their visitors and readers read your content on their websites, they will most likely reach out to you to find out more and eventually become a customer.

Guest blogging is time-consuming. Do it the right way, this way, so you don't waste a lot of time:

1. Identify the companies with the same prospects as you.

2. Create a dream list of 10-15 brands to start with, and approach them every month with a new content suggestion.

3. Make a personalised approach and propose three relevant topics for their audience.

4. Follow up at least three times.

5. When approved, write your blog post with:

    a. a concise author bio

    b. links that redirect to your website

    c. a great call to action that will push them to act right now.

Budget: 0 to £

Complexity: Hire a copywriter or do it yourself

Time required: Few days

SECTION 3:

Building trust, credibility and your prospect list

Strategy 12 - Email list build-up

Building your mailing list, wherever you have a B2B or B2C business, is still crucial. Your mailing list allows you to have a connection with the community outside of social media platforms.

What unique value will people get for being on your mailing list? It's the most important question you need to ask yourself before you start building your mailing list. They should be tailored for your specific audience with valuable content. If you have different target audiences, split your audiences into various lists.

How to build your mailing list:

- What can you give your audience that they will find of value? This could be creating an e-guide, a report, free emojis, or anything else.

- Use your social media platforms to spread the word. With a paid social media campaign, you will grow your mailing list much faster. If your budget is limited, be creative with social media communication by utilising stories, hashtags, partnerships, commenting on other accounts, and replying to all messages you receive.

Budget: 0 to £

Complexity: Easy

Time required: Less than an hour

Strategy 13 – Pop it up

Have you ever visited a website and within a second a pop-up comes on screen, requesting you to leave your email address? It can be irritating, but why does everyone do it? It works, but most of the time, brands don't use them effectively.

The website pop-up is a great way to build your mailing list, and yes, it does work. We have grown our mailing by 2,000 in six months using a pop-up. Why do these things work when so many people complain about them? Most importantly, how do you make sure it works for your business?

Pop-ups have to be seen to be closed; therefore, content blindness doesn't occur with them. To make it work for you, make sure they don't pop out as soon as your visitors are on your website. They should pop-up when your visitor intends to exit your page or after a couple of minutes.

Pop-ups are a great strategy to engage your visitors where you can reward them with a discount or free guide in exchange for their email address.

Budget: 0

Complexity: Easy

Time required: Less than an hour

Strategy 14 – Success stories

As I mentioned previously, we are risk-averse by nature. So, when dealing with a business we are not familiar with, we are sceptical. We often look to be reassured by knowing other people have tried and obtained successful results with a brand. The main purpose of case studies is first, to reinforce your credibility and second, to reassure a prospect that your brand is a safe choice. Case studies show potential clients exactly what you can do for them.

Would you rather I tell you a story or tell you what I do? I bet you prefer the story and, to be honest, me too. We love stories, so take your prospects on a journey telling the stories of the individuals or companies you have worked with. Case studies written like success stories stimulate their mind and desire to experience the same.

Case studies are part of the discovery phase. Your job is to convince them since this is when a prospect will decide to buy from you or enquire to find out more. The founder of Ring, the video doorbell company, was acquired by Amazon for one billion dollars despite being previously rejected by investors on Shark Tank, the American TV show. Their Instagram page showcases real stories of how customers have used their product to send away thieves and burglars or record acts of kindness or happiness.

How to make your case studies engaging, which means make prospects contact you or buy from you:

- Write case studies that speak directly to your potential clients' challenges and desires.
- Add as many keywords as you can through your content to bring in organic search traffic. For example, if you run a sales consultancy firm for technology companies, use words such as technology, sales etc. Use words and sentences your audience is most likely to search for online.

- Reach out to your existing clients and find out if you can get some positive qualitative and quantitative information as a result of working with you. If you can ask for clients to deliver their feedback in a video format, that is even better.

- Each case study should be presented as a success story. First, present the problem they were facing before choosing your products or services. This is where you articulate the pains and challenges that relate to the prospect who is reading this. Second, present the products or services they chose or the work you did to help them resolve their issues. Finally, present the results they were able to achieve and the feelings these have brought into their life. Complete your story with your client testimonials and invite prospects to take action.

- Publish and promote your success stories online and in conversations.

Budget: 0

Complexity: Easy

Time required: Continuously

Strategy 15 – Ebook

The ebook, my favourite. Since launching my business, I have written hundreds of ebooks that have been downloaded by thousands of people. Ebooks are so great because they help you grow your mailing list, build credibility, and upsell your services or products. We don't like to be sold to, but we love to buy. Don't we? Before buying, we want to make sure we are buying from the right business or individual. Using the ebook approach is a great strategy to offer a sample of your knowledge.

How to write an ebook:

- Do you know that you already have the content of your ebook? Yes, you do. If you have been writing blog posts or articles, compile them in an organised manner to create an ebook.

- If you have never written anything, that's OK. Ask yourself, what are the most common questions your target audience asks? For example, here are some questions a personal trainer who works with women will often get:

  o How do I get rid of cellulite?

  o How do I lose belly fat?

  o How do I get a bigger butt?

"Get my ebook and discover how to tone your body with my fitness programme targeting cellulite, belly fat, and butt. I have added yummy recipes to make in 10 minutes. See results in 14 days, and you don't need any equipment." Does it sound like an ebook you would like to read? Of course! Run an ad campaign like that and see your mailing list grow exponentially.

What should you include in your ebook?

Through your content, add links to videos, client case studies, testimonials, your website, and contact details. Present yourself or your team with a strong bio to emphasise your authority. This is a great opportunity to upsell. To maximise conversion, combine your ebook with an email automation campaign where you can provide limited offers for new subscribers; make sure the offer has a deadline.

Writing it is not enough; you need to promote it!

No one will find your ebook if you don't promote it. That's the part most entrepreneurs neglect; the broadcasting.

- Create a landing page with your SEO keywords so search engines can start recommending your page.
- Share your ebook on your social media pages and with relevant influencers.
- Promote your ebook through your social media pages and website.
- Allow people to share your landing page.
- Track success continuously.

Budget: £

Complexity: Hire an expert or do it yourself

Time required: Few days

Strategy 16 – Whitepapers

OK, whitepapers. They are a little more advanced than ebooks. What is the difference between a whitepaper and an ebook? Whitepapers are, by nature, more "serious" than ebooks. They are influential, in-depth, and persuasive reports that present a market issue or issues. A whitepaper will also present a suitable solution or discuss a particular methodology.

Whitepapers give you an opportunity to position your brand as a market influencer and even leader. They are often referred to by journalists. It is more than a database building. It is also a great PR tool when used effectively.

How to write a whitepaper:

1. Identify a market issue that your target audience and industry find of relevance. For example, post-Brexit brand and marketing challenges UK tech businesses should be prepared for? The subject is relevant, on-topic, and specific to various stakeholders. Carry out as much research as possible, so you leave no room for assumptions, then write about it in great depth.

2. When you present the challenges, the aim is to present your brand as one of the natural solutions to resolve these challenges. Weave your products or services into your writing and explain how they can benefit your reader.

3. The tone of voice should remain professional and confident to leave no room for doubt.

4. Make sure to get it proofread.

Remember that's not it, you need to promote it:

1. Find 10-15 journalists who are likely to be interested in this topic and send it to them

2. Promote your whitepaper as I taught you with your ebook in chapter 15.

Budget: 0

Complexity: You are the expert

Time required: Few weeks

Strategy 17 – Infographics

An image is worth a thousand words. If you operate in a busy market, you need to find creative ways to differentiate yourself from your competition. Infographics are an excellent way to do so. But what are they? They are visual content. They are advice or insightful information presented through illustrations. Infographic marketing is a great opportunity for your brand to present information in a dynamic and visual format which is distinctive from your competitors. Great infographics are often reshared and build your brand awareness exponentially.

How to create a great infographic:

- Choose a topic that is relevant to your target audience, but that will also educate them.
- Save your image with the right keywords and use the right hashtags when sharing.
- Brand your infographic and add your brand details so it can be traced back to you.
- Allow your content to be shareable to drive traffic.

Budget: £

Complexity: Hire a graphic designer

Time required: Few days

Strategy 18 - Video tutorials

Video tutorials are still extremely effective because people love to watch, as it requires the least effort. It is better to watch a video tutorial about how to make a vegan carrot cake than read instructions. If you sell a ready cake mix, create video tutorials to show various ways to decorate the cake or use it as a base to make various cakes. Video tutorials are an effective marketing strategy to drive sales while building your fan base. A great video tutorial allows you to add your personality. People buy people, remember, so let them fall in love with you.

So, use video tutorials to simplify complex tasks into something that's easy to pick up and understand. If you sell products such as makeup, tech products, building tools, food recipes, show your potential customers how to best use your products or "do like you." If you are camera shy, work with social influencers as your brand ambassadors.

How to best prepare a video tutorial:

- Prepare your video tutorial by breaking down the sections you want to cover.
- Add your personality when recording because you aren't a robot.
- Don't forget to tell your viewers what to do next: subscribe, like, and where they can get your products or contact you.

Budget: 0 to £

Complexity: Do it yourself or hire a video editor

Time required: Few hours

Strategy 19 Online course

Are you confused about this? Are you wondering why you should create an online course to get customers? Remember, knowledge and experience you have accumulated over the years might be gold for someone else out there. If your business growth is limited by the time you have at your disposal, online courses are excellent to scale without working 24 hours a day. Get paid to share your knowledge.

You can have a free online course to use it as a hook to get prospects to sign up to your paid products or services. You can also have paid courses for prospects who "do it yourself" as they can't yet afford your services. The free course may also be used to generate leads for a paid course. When they enter your sales funnel, it is easier to upsell higher services and products as you would have used your free course to prove your credibility.

Having a course can also position you as an industry leader and get you more personal brand exposure.

How to get started:

1. Write your content in a PowerPoint presentation format.
2. Record yourself talking through each slide.
3. Add key takeaways and exercises.
4. Promote it continuously.

Budget: £

Complexity: Hire a web developer

Time required: Few weeks

Strategy 20 – Automate your emails

Email automation workflows are automated emails that you can send to help nurture your leads into customers. Automation is only as good as the person who creates it. So, if you don't know how to do it, it will deliver poor results. Email automation allows you to automate repetitive communication to ensure prospects or clients get the same brand experience. Email automation is only effective if your lists are effectively segmented. It is useful if your business deals with a large number of customers which would make it time-consuming and ineffective to create individual, personal emails.

How and when to use email automation?

While building your mailing list, think about what you would like your email subscribers to know about you to build trust and credibility so they can decide to be a customer. You should have a series of emails that get delivered over the first seven to ten days after they subscribed to your mailing list. Don't make the mistakes to send too many emails every day. You will turn your warm leads into cold leads.

They are more likely to buy from you if you engage immediately. Remember we have a short attention span, so don't get forgotten.

1. Your first email should be a welcome message accompanied with the gift you promised to give in your campaign.

2. Your next emails should focus on the following elements:

   a. More valuable content that redirects to your website or video content.

   b. Invitation to engage directly or on social media.

   c. Client stories.

   d. Company presentation.

   e. Call to action: Book a call, special offers, etc.

When well-orchestrated, in the long run, you will save time and costs and eradicate errors other people may have made.

Here is my guide to developing a successful automated email campaign:

a. Define your audience and goals from the start so you can measure the success of your campaign effectively.

b. To avoid your email going into the spam folder, avoid spammy words such as "buy now."

c. You will have a higher open rate if you add the name of your reader in the subject line and the body of your email. So, get personal.

d. Stop thinking like a marketer and write like a human. Think about a friend when writing your copy, so it speaks to them.

e. Don't overdo it with images and videos; sometimes less is more.

Budget: £

Complexity: Hire an expert or do it yourself

Time required: Few weeks

Strategy 21 – A newsletter

You cannot automate your entire email communication, and this is where the newsletter comes into play as part of your nurturing phase. After completion of your email automation, your newsletter provides updates about your brand, products, and services. If you use your newsletter for the hard sell, you will reduce your open rate and lose subscribers. Instead, use it to share interesting updates about your brand, and naturally, your prospects will be curious to find out more.

For example, if you are a fashion brand, provide tips on how to dress for summer by creating looks from your new collection. If you are a law firm, provide tips regarding new regulations and how to avoid trouble; naturally, your prospects will be more likely to get in touch to find out more. Don't hesitate to encourage your readers to take action with a call to action; e.g. find out more or contact us if you have further questions.

Newsletters are underestimated and are still crucial in marketing campaigns. They are still more effective than social media. So, don't ghost your subscribers and regularly stay in touch with them.

Tips for creating a successful email newsletter:

- Keep your newsletter short and to the point.
- Choose a catchy subject line to ensure it will incite your subscribers to open it.
- Do an A/B test and see if your newsletter gets a better open rate with or without visuals. Don't forget to also test different time.
- Always add a call to action.
- Add social media links to allow your subscribers to share your newsletter.
- Measure the success of your email newsletter (open rate, click rate, etc).

Budget: £

Complexity: Easy

Time required: A few hours

Strategy 22 - Trials

Are you offering innovative products or services that are not familiar to your potential customers, or require a long commitment? A free trial is still an effective marketing strategy. You can attract potential customers who don't know your product while removing their financial risk. Free trials allow you to increase prospect conversion, product adoption, and customer loyalty. You can also attract more customers and accumulate good reviews and testimonials in the process.

Remember we are, by nature, risk averse. So, when dealing with a business we aren't familiar with, we are looking for safety and guarantees so we don't make a mistake that may cost us money.

Have you ever watched the TV show Hell's Kitchen with Gordon Ramsay? It follows a British chef who swears uncontrollably at terrible restaurant owners on the verge of bankruptcy. After revamping their restaurants to bring sceptical customers back in, he stands outside and offers food samples. When they sample the food, one in three will make a reservation or dine in straightaway.

Offering a trial or sample is a great way to get people to discover your products or services without engagement. The goal is to get them hooked, so they choose to stay. Why do you think car dealers always take you on a test drive or tech companies always offer a fourteen-day trial? It works. You can learn a lot from Zoom and Slack success.

Budget: 0 to £

Complexity: Easy

Time required: Few days for set up

Strategy 23 – Giveaways

Giveaways are a great way to bring attention to what you do, but they need to be done effectively to avoid attracting freebie hunters.

Here is what you need to do to make it work for your brand:

1. Start by defining the goal of your giveaway. Is it to grow your mailing list? Generate sales volume? Build brand awareness? Set up the correct KPIs to keep yourself aligned with your goals.

2. Have amazing prizes to win and make it easy to participate. If your prize isn't worth the time to complete a form or submit your details, you are setting yourself up for failure. Offer something worth stopping for. Have you ever seen the competition to win a sports car at the airport? I don't know the exact rules, but it is worth buying a ten-pound lottery ticket to have the chance to win a luxury sports car. I have seen a lot of men falling for it particularly. The car is shiny, men get to sit in it, and in a fraction of second, thousands of people around the world have purchased a ticket. The strategy is effective and works!

3. Target your ideal audience thoroughly. One goal should be to obtain the details of potential customers with whom you can carry on nurturing the relationship. So, in your data collection strategy, allow yourself to filter out people who will don't match your target audience.

4. To double or triple your brand awareness, nothing is stopping you from partnering with other brands, celebrities, or influencers. Movie productions often work with social influencers to creatively promote a new film. It is effective, and it works if you share the same target audience.

Budget: £ to £££
Complexity: Easy
Time required: Few weeks

Strategy 24 – Podcast

As you know by now, I have my own podcast, *Tech Brains Talk*, where I interview extraordinary entrepreneurs and leaders in the world of tech. This has helped me grow my brand awareness within technology and also attract my ideal clients.

Podcast reach is a natural addition to your inbound marketing activities. Podcasts have become part of our daily life. We listen in the morning, on the tube, behind the wheel of a car, or in the shower. With millions of listeners every day, it is a great business opportunity for you to boost engagement, trust with prospects, increase likability, and generate leads.

How to launch your podcast

- Determine the focus of your podcast. It needs to be relevant to your prospects, so create content that resonates with your niche.
- Invite potential prospects and interview key influencers in your industry who your prospects would love to listen to.
- Get yourself a nice microphone to get the best sound.
- Use a podcast recording platform and host your podcast episodes
- Prep your guest by sending a few questions. Record it and get it edited.
- Promote: If no one knows, no will listen. Ask your guests to promote it as well. They are more likely to promote if you create some personalised visuals to go along their podcast interview.

Budget: 0 to £

Complexity: Hire a graphic designer or sound editor

Time required: Few days

SECTION 4:

Social media communication

Strategy 25 - Facebook business page

This sounds so obvious, but so many businesses haven't set up their Facebook Business Page. What? Yes, you read this right. 1.67 billion users are logging on to Facebook every single day. Can you see the money? You could reach prospective clients halfway across the world, as easily as you could reach your local community with Facebook Ads.

Facebook business page features will also give you valuable insight into your audience, such as the number of page views, post reactions, the demographic of your followers, and many more insights. So, you use your beautiful fingers and get yourself on Facebook.

How to use a Facebook business page to get customers:

- On your page header, add a video, it grabs people's attention.
- Add links to all your other pages.
- Write a bio with all your keywords so Facebook can rank your page.
- You can schedule your post directly on Facebook.
- If you sell tangible products, link them to your website.
- Start a live video when you have reached enough followers.
- Brag about your success as often as you can.
- Publish events; this is super important as this feature is often used by Facebook users.
- Promote your page to your network to get more followers.

Budget: 0

Complexity: Easy

Time required: Continuously

Strategy 26 – Facebook private group

Did you know that there are around 620 million Facebook groups? Facebook groups are the perfect place for your followers, prospects, or customers to interact with each other and for you to build brand loyalty. If you consistently interact with your audience, this will give your business a personal touch, and they form an emotional connection with the brand and stay loyal, even when the business makes mistakes. Followers can also leave reviews and feedback, which can be used to improve your business and make it more appealing to attract your prospects.

Tips for creating a Facebook group:

- Make the rules clear. Don't be too strict with too many don'ts as it will kill the desire to engage.

- Use a different themed discussion on a weekly basis.

How to effectively use a Facebook private group

- Create your own Facebook group and invite your existing clients to join in. Then give them a perk for recommending anyone to the group. Remember, your clients tend to be around people who are like them, so ask them to recommend you.

- If you don't have any clients yet, create a business challenge and invite your network to participate in a prize draw. Your prize could be one of your services and/or products.

- Do a joint venture with another business who serves the same type of customers and give them a commission or cross-sell your offers. The way you present your brand is extremely important. So, don't neglect your shop window. Make sure you have an attractive value proposition, and your business presentation is breath-taking.

- Don't want to create your own Facebook group? No problem. Join other Facebook groups but don't do like so many people and spam, talking about what you do. Instead, take the time to read what people are sharing and provide advice. With social media, it is always about providing value first. So, educate, advise, and, if you have something you can give for free, that is even better.

Budget: 0

Complexity: Easy

Time required: Continuously

Strategy 27 – Facebook marketplace

Facebook marketplace is very similar to Gumtree. If you are looking for a convenient way to sell tangible items locally, this is perfect for you. It is ideal for selling end of season items, for example. The Facebook browsing feature will optimise to display your items to potential buyers based on their location. It helps save your business time trying to optimise yourself.

How to win customers using Facebook marketplace:

- An image speaks a thousand words, so make sure to use the best photos to present your products.
- Spend some time writing a compelling product description with a price and your location.
- Cross-promote on your Facebook page and group, if you have one.

Budget: 0

Complexity: Easy

Time required: Continuously

Strategy 28 – Twitter

Twitter for business is another great social media platform that can be used to promote your brand. According to statistics from Twitter, the platform had over 300 million users in 2019, and these users send over 150 million tweets a day. The platform has become notorious for being the place where networking occurs, and conversations take place, as it allows normal people to interact with large organisations, celebrities, and people worldwide, all within 280 characters.

Statistics by Hootsuite state that 79% of Twitter users have retweeted a small to medium-sized business at least once. Unlike other platforms, since Twitter allows tweets to be accessed by anyone searching, even those without an account, the content of the tweet is more likely to be seen by the target audience. The platform also makes it easier to share multiple types of media, such as ebooks, blogs, and lead magnets, therefore making it easier for potential consumers to access your content.

Tips for creating a great Tweet that gets noticed:

- Discover trendy topics, for example, #Brexit #TechWeek are the current trending topics, then find a way to connect these trendy topics to your activities in one tweet.

- Identify the influencers in your industry or individuals to tag in your tweets too. The goal is for them to respond, like, or even retweet so you can grow your brand awareness.

- Write your tweet about your business while integrating different trends. For example, @3ColoursRule is at #TechWeek. Read our article brand strategy to thrive after #Brexit. What do you think, @PrinceHarry?

Budget: 0

Complexity: Easy

Time required: Continuously

Strategy 29 – Pinterest

Pinterest, best known for recipes, fashion, and home design ideas, has become so much more today. Pinterest is the top visual search engine. When you use search engines to discover visuals, it often takes you back to a Pinterest post.

If visuals are crucial in convincing your prospects to buy your products or services, you should be on Pinterest. So, start posting photography or original graphics. Pinterest is an excellent platform to drive traffic to your website. Most users use Pinterest to find photos of new products and the platform, so make sure to use the right keywords to describe each of your photos. Remember, Pinterest is about visuals, but for you, it will be an SEO exercise to get discovered.

How to get started on Pinterest:

1. Create your brand profile:

- Ensure your bio best describes the uniqueness of your brand.
- Upload your brand logo.
- Choose your cover board, so it best represents what you do.
- Create five showcase boards that are aligned with what you do.
- Brand your board covers so we can recognise your brand.
- Verify your website.

2. Determine your content strategy:

Your objective is to provide great visual content that will help you rank on search engines and be shared by others on Pinterest. Think about the top business challenges of your audience.

3. Join community boards where your prospects and influencers are most likely to be so you can connect with them and build rapport.

4. Focus on using the right descriptions and keywords. Your Pinterest SEO must be strong.

5. Post regularly and schedule new pins so you can grow your followers.

Budget: 0

Complexity: Easy

Time required: Continuously

Strategy 30 - Instagram

Did you know that 72% of Instagram users make a purchase decision after seeing something on Instagram?

Instagram is one of the most popular social platforms to get you leads and take your sales to the next level. Instagram has added many features to help you grow businesses and makes it easy for users to purchase from your posts and links. But there is more to it than just creating a post, sharing it, and expecting users to purchase from you.

In 2018, Instagram released three main factors that affect the visibility of your posts and how the algorithm perceives them:

- **Interest:** The more Instagram thinks that the user is going to like the post, the higher Instagram ranks it in their feed.

- **Timeliness:** Instagram does not want to prioritise content from a week ago. Instead, they would prefer to prioritise new content. That way, it encourages Instagram page owners to keep posting regularly.

- **Relationship:** You will need to constantly monitor your followers to see when they are active and post then.

How to get customers from Instagram:

- A visual presentation is important. Take the time to create a great visual flow.

- Be consistent with your posting. You don't have to post every day but posting once a month won't get you far.

- Use Instagram stories to engage with quizzes, polls etc.

- Create an Instagram story group with whom you can share some exclusive stories.

- Use your hashtags. You can use up to 30 hashtags. When it comes to hashtags, don't pick the most popular ones as you will compete with too many users trying to get to the top. Instead, choose hashtags with medium popularity to increase exposure.

- Tag yourself and any person or relevant brand, so they engage.
- Add your location.
- Last the not the least, engage. Comment and like regularly on pages that you follow. The power of reciprocity will increase engagement on your page.

Budget: 0

Complexity: Easy to moderate

Time required: Continuously

Strategy 31 – SlideShare

Do you give talks and presentations? Well, use SlideShare to be discovered by your audience. SlideShare, which now belongs to LinkedIn, is known among professionals. You can upload a sample or the whole PowerPoint presentation. It is often overlooked and not used in the customer acquisition strategy.

SlideShare is ideal for B2B businesses, and you should share:

- Educational content. Only post a sample of your presentation and invite viewers to subscribe to your newsletter or submit their details on your landing page to receive the full presentation. This will help you build your mailing list and identify prospects.

- Company presentation. You can upload the full presentation

Budget: 0

Complexity: You are the expert

Time required: Few days

Strategy 32 - TikTok

Did you know that TikTok was the most downloaded app in January 2020? With 800 million active users, it is bigger than Twitter and Pinterest! Do I have your attention now? The chances of finding prospects on TikTok are pretty good. Do you still think TikTok is not for you?

Most businesses that do not target Millennials or Gen Z believe TikTok is not for them. But we have seen a growing number of more mature users joining the platform. To win the TikTok game, you have to engage with your potential customers through entertainment.

How to attract customers using TikTok:

1. Start by creating your brand channel and upload some of your existing videos.

2. Check out what is trending and join the wave to gain new followers.

3. Identify relevant influencers and focus on getting them to share your content with their broader audience; choosing your influencers is key as you need to get the right target attention.

4. You may also consider advertising to increase the engagement of your ad campaign. If you are new to TikTok, don't spend more than 10% of your marketing budget.

Budget: 0

Complexity: Easy to moderate

Time required: Continuously

Strategy 33 - LinkedIn profile page

LinkedIn is, by far, my favourite social media platform. LinkedIn is different from the other platforms as it is, first and foremost, a business to business platform where professionals can connect. LinkedIn has over 450 million users and millions of millionaires using this platform regularly. If you ever type your full name on search engines, your LinkedIn profile will appear in the top search results. LinkedIn is also a great SEO tool to be discovered by potential prospects.

How to use LinkedIn effectively to attract customers:

- Add a professional photo and a background that showcases your expertise.
- Keywords. Think about the keywords your prospects are most likely to search online to find someone with your expertise. Then, add those keywords into your biography and role descriptions.
- Add relevant work experience and present what you have achieved within each role. Add visuals when you can.
- Add any interviews, videos, awards/nominations you may have won.
- Join LinkedIn groups where your prospects might be, but also to increase your network reach.
- Make a habit of posting regularly. Your content should be educational, motivational, inspirational, or entertaining, but not like Facebook
- Ask for recommendations from clients, colleagues, partners and any relevant stakeholders who will improve your credibility

Budget: 0

Complexity: Easy

Time required: Continuously

Strategy 34 – LinkedIn business page

We often discover a business online before we meet the team behind the brand. This means how we present our business matters. Having a LinkedIn company page is a great way to establish your brand credibility and share what you do and who you serve.

When you add your company name to your LinkedIn personal profile, they are now hyperlinked, and it makes it easy for anyone to discover your company name and learn more about your brand.

Your LinkedIn business page is different from your LinkedIn profile page. It should focus on your company activities and the team as a whole. By creating a company page, you multiply the chances of being discovered by your target audience. Why? When users perform a search, they can also search by company name to review the employees. Google previews up to 156 characters of your page text, so make sure your description has the right keywords by including words that describe your business, expertise, and industry focus. Also use it to attract and engage quality candidates with feature videos, employee testimonials, and more.

What should you share on your LinkedIn company page?

- Share company stories (charity, new employees, awards, etc.).
- Share your vision, mission and success milestones.
- Share industry insights to demonstrate your brand is knowledgeable and therefore trustworthy.
- Share your purpose and what are you doing for your community.

Budget: 0

Complexity: Easy

Time required: Continuously

Strategy 35 – YouTube

YouTube has become the most popular platform for video content. Video content is a great medium for delivering your branded value proposition. More and more businesses are adding video marketing as part of their prospecting strategy. If you want to reach different generations of users, YouTube can take your business to the next level. Creating your own YouTube channel is the right place to start. 82% of B2C businesses choose YouTube as their preferred platform to interact with their customers. YouTube is a great platform to engage with a young generation as they are avid users.

However, there are a few things that you should do when you create a YouTube channel:

- Add your logo and give your channel a unique look.
- Accept feedback and engage with your audience.
- Be consistent and create a video content schedule to make sure you post regularly.
- Always have a CTA: subscribe, like, and/or comment.
- Always transcribe your videos. Search engines cannot trawl your videos. This is why it is crucial to have the transcript so your videos can be indexed and ranked. A transcript makes your video more searchable across the web and will therefore increase traffic, link building opportunities, and see your search rankings improve.
- Add keywords and as much description to each video as you can to maximise discovery.

Budget: 0

Complexity: Easy to moderate

Time required: Continuously

Strategy 36 – Reddit

If you have ever visited Reddit's website, you have probably said to yourself, "This looks like a complete mess of memes, self-posts, and baby pictures." Despite all this, Reddit remains a good site to promote your business on and discover valuable information. For Reddit to work for you, you need to get to the front page.

How to do it:

- Create a subreddit.
- Post helpful, informative, and/or hilarious content.
- Be consistent by being an active user.
- Raise awareness and engagement by participating in an AMA (Ask Me Anything).

Budget: 0

Complexity: Moderate to difficult

Time required: Continuously

Strategy 37 – Quora

If you haven't heard about Quora, where have you been? Did you know that Quora was founded by a Facebook CTO? It attracts not only your potential customers but also journalists and industry insiders keen to answer millions of questions for free.

To maximise the potential of your business on Quora, try the following:

1. Create an account and complete your profile in detail.

2. Look for questions within your expertise that you can answer.

3. Ask questions to open the lines of communication.

4. Follow other users and connect with them to grow your network.

Budget: 0

Complexity: Easy

Time required: Continuously

Strategy 38 - Social influencers

It is interesting how "influencer" has become a positive word. With the rise of social media, consumers tend to blindly trust influencers and the products and brands they recommend. They have managed to grow very engaged audiences that you can access. When you partner with influencers to promote your brand or products, their followers may end up purchasing from you.

You may not have a budget to get Dwayne Johnson or Kim Kardashian to talk about your brand, but there are many social influencers you can work with. If you can't offer to pay social influencers, work with micro-influencers (fewer followers but still engaged ones) with whom you can offer a commission structure. Make sure your commission is great, so they feel incentivised to support your campaign.

Tips for creating a successful social influencer strategy:

- Define your goals - What is success for you? What do you want to achieve?
- Select relevant influencers.
- Send a personalised pitch and follow up at least twice.
- Design your campaign with each influencer. They are creative individuals, so give them some creative space while providing with your brand guidelines.
- Track and optimise.
- Build great relationships with each influencer, and you will achieve great results.

Budget: 0 to £££

Complexity: Moderate

Time required: Continuously

Strategy 39 - Blog forums

Blogs and forums are still very relevant as the audience is very targeted. It is similar to posting on private social media platforms. Sharing valuable content by posting on local area blog forums is a quick and excellent way to get your message across to your targeted audience. If your business operation is geographically limited, this is a great strategy if you are looking to communicate with your local communities.

To acquire customers with this strategy:

- Select your niche blog forums.
- Engage regularly by posting, commenting and sharing valuable content.
- Connect with users and invite to join your community.

Budget: 0

Complexity: Easy to Moderate

Time required: Continuously

SECTION 5:

PR for credibility and lead conversion

Strategy 40 – Journalists

Getting the attention of journalists will get your brand noticed, raise your brand credibility, and facilitate the conversion from prospects to customers. When this happens, it's a great bonus. The question is, how?

Do you know who is interested in what you do?

Blasting press releases to a list of journalists won't get you noticed and won't get your business in the press. So, do your research.

- Pick a couple of media outlets where you would like your business to appear. Find 10-15 journalists and influencers you believe would be interested in writing about you.

- Use Twitter. It is a great tool to connect with all the journalists and influencers in your industry. Follow them and engage by asking them what they like to write about even if it is obvious. 80% of the time, they will respond.

It's all about your story

Journalists only care about a great brand story, not your business. Ask yourself the following questions:

- Why do you do what you do?
- How does your company impact others?
- Who works with you? What's your company culture?
- Is your company's approach different from your competitors? If yes, what is the positive impact?
- Can your company story inspire others?
- Is your business innovative or original to what is available in the market?
- Do you go beyond your product and service offering to support your customers?

By answering those questions, you will be able to write a great brand story that journalists would want to write about. So, get started! You will improve, but only if you start!

Budget: 0

Complexity: Moderate

Time required: Continuously

Strategy 41 – Newspapers

Some say newspapers are dead. Well, for sure, newspapers are not the same as they used to be in the 70s. The average newspaper circulation has been in constant decline as we have found easier ways to consume information online rather than via traditional newspapers.

Despite all of the above, it is worth it; let me tell you why:

- If you offer locally based products or services, this is a great way to promote your brand in an affordable way. Plus, the chance of getting a great placement is higher as there will be less competition.
- There is something different about seeing your brand or your name in a tangible newspaper. No online media has that same impact. When you appear in the newspaper, take a photo and post it online to raise your brand credibility.
- It is still a great way to build your brand credibility and therefore, brand attractiveness.
- Most newspapers offer a digital version, so always ask to be covered in both.
- If you have an incredible story to share, approach the right journalists, so you don't have to pay for advertising.

Budget: 0

Complexity: Easy to difficult

Time required: Continuously

Strategy 42 – Radio

Not enough attention is given to radio as a medium. Radio is the perfect middle ground between newspaper and podcast.

How to get customers using the radio strategy:

- Be a guest on a radio programme. Apply the same approach I shared in strategy 40 to get yourself on the radio.

- Radio advertising is often forgotten or perceived as pricey by most businesses. However, radio advertising has an influence on its listeners whether we notice it or not. If you are familiar with my neuromarketing talks, I often talk about subconscious decision making. If you listen to the radio regularly, you have unconsciously purchased a product or a service after hearing an advertisement on the radio. For best results, your radio campaign should last at least three months.

Budget: 0 to £££

Complexity: Moderate - You will need to hire a radio advertising agency

Time required: Continuously

Strategy 43 – Online magazine

Magazines aren't as popular as they used to be because of digitisation, but that doesn't mean that we don't read anymore. Online magazines can be an excellent way to reach new audiences while developing advertising revenue. To be effective, you have to put together content your audience is interested in. The content should be a mix: educative, entertaining and original content. It allows you to drive direct customers and advertisers in the same instance.

To maximise your reach, integrate Google Analytics, link to your website and/or selling ad space. With advertising, you have now created another new revenue stream for your business.

How to create a great online magazine

1. Determine the business objectives for your online magazine from the start. What is your unique value? Then create an action plan to achieve your goals.

2. Define your brand style, so your brand is quickly recognisable.

3. Now work on your content. How can you make your content engaging and actionable? With a digital magazine format, use interactive features to create an engaging experience for your readers. Add galleries, audio, and video content with clickable and shopping cart buttons.

4. When everything is proofread, you are ready to publish. Use all the publication platforms available to maximise your reach. Reach out to all stakeholders from journalists, influencers, and bloggers to your prospects and clients.

5. Always track. If you want to sell advertising space or just stay apprised of the effectiveness of this strategy, use analytic software. The data you collect will become useful when creating future issues.

Budget: 0 to £

Complexity: Hire a graphic designer or use a self-design platform

Time required: Few days

Strategy 44 – Awards

Everyone wants to walk with winners, and winning awards will increase your credibility and attractiveness when you stand among your competitors. When you win an award, people start paying attention to who you are and what you do. It opens doors to new business opportunities and high-profile networks. If you think you aren't good enough or haven't accomplished enough, that's OK. Still apply, as getting nominated is a stepping-stone. You will attract better clients, better employees, the media, investors, and so much more.

What type of awards can you apply for?

1. Evaluate all the categories you and your company can fit into. This could be geographical, location, diversity, gender, impact, etc.

2. Check out the leaders in your market and identify the awards they have won so you can apply as well this year or next year.

3. Make a list, so you don't miss annual deadlines.

4. Now evaluate what you and your company have accomplished, and don't underestimate your milestones.

5. If you are nominated, let everyone know, offline and online, as it is already a great achievement.

6. Keep trying until you win this award.

Budget: 0 to £££

Complexity: Easy to moderate

Time required: Continuously

Strategy 45 – Celebrity clients

One of humankind's characteristics is to avoid risk and copy what others do if we believe it is a safe choice. The best advertising for your business is word of mouth. It is amplified when it comes from the mouth of celebrity clients. Let them do the talking, both online and offline.

You should target to work with the most recognised celebrities. Celebrities can be the most high-profile companies or individuals. This will increase your credibility, prospect requests, and, consequently, customer acquisition. The more celebrity brands and individuals you have under your belt, the easier it becomes to attract customers.

How to secure celebrity customers to attract more customers:

1. Make a list of the top 20 brands you would love to work with and do your research, so you identify their current challenges.

2. Position your business as the expert that is missing for them to achieve their vision. Identify their challenges and present a theoretical solution. I mean don't give solutions for free, but present methods. Let me give you a B2B example. Diversity is a big issue in advertising; most brands don't understand how to communicate to the black community, gen z or generation alpha. In my case, the way I would approach a brand I want to work with is by highlighting the untapped opportunities within one of these groups, and the work I have done in the past to engage with them. Politely present why they haven't achieved this and how you can help them.

3. Be creative and original with your approach. As you may guess, they are both highly demanding and demanded individuals, so be different to catch their attention

4. When they have become a customer of your brand, let the world know through both offline and online communication channels.

Budget: 0 to ££

Complexity: Easy to moderate

Time required: Continuously

SECTION 6:

Prospecting and advertising

Strategy 46 - A/B test

Test, test, and test! Did I say that enough? I'm not sure, as I often see marketers, entrepreneurs, and business owners launch one version of their campaign and hope for the best. Wherever you create landing pages, write email copy, do an ad campaign, or design call-to-action buttons, don't just follow your intuition and assume things will work. You need to create variations of your content and design, then evaluate which one generates the most engagement and conversion before allocating your full budget.

A/B testing is when you create different campaigns to direct traffic to your website, landing page, or something else. It consists of splitting your campaigns and serving them to different groups of people, then evaluating which campaigns performed best. When you can clearly identify the best performing campaign, allocate your resources to that and cancel the other ones.

For example, you can have two different campaigns, but change one of the following factors: copy, font, image, target audience, etc. If you change more than one factor, you won't be able to identify what the differentiator is. So, it is best to launch multiple A/B test campaigns with just one-factor alteration. Launch your A/B campaigns and wait and see which campaigns perform better.

Bad marketers make decisions based on feeling and guesswork. You won't be one as you are reading this book. Instead, use the A/B testing strategy to remove any assumptions and make decisions based on solid results.

How to conduct an A/B design test:

1. Determine the goal of your campaign.
2. Specify your A/B test budget from the start.
3. Change only one factor.
4. Test at least two different factors.

5. Take a sample of your prospect list, split your sample into two groups equally and randomly. Make you your sample size sufficient so you can get enough data to proceed to the next phase.

6. Review the results, score your campaign, and keep the best one.

Budget: ££

Complexity: Get trained or Hire an expert

Time required: Few weeks

Strategy 47 - Google AdWords

The dream of any business is to be discovered by their clients on search engines. You have created this fabulous website with great content and enquiries are continuously coming in. That's the dream, and this can be achieved with SEO (search engine optimisation), but sometimes it can take forever when you need prospects to reach out to you now. If you don't have the luxury of waiting, that's when Google AdWords comes in.

If you are not yet ranking on the first page on a search engine, don't worry, as this is pretty common and that's why Google created Google AdWords to rank on top of the organic search.

How to achieve success out of Google AdWords:

1. Do your keyword research.

- What are the popular keywords or phrases your prospects use to search for your service? For example, avoid personal trainers in London, instead, choose personal trainers in Clapham. The more targeted you are, the more prospects you will convert.

- Think about your customer journey. Where are they? What common question searches are your prospects likely to perform online? For example: What exercises to do when your back is sore? With this type of question research, you can, for example, direct them to an ebook and capture their email address. Basically, carry out an ad campaign at the pre-buying phase, ready to explore phase, and ready to buy phase.

2. Test, test, test with A/B test

Keep your ad KISS (Keep It Simple & Straightforward). It should articulate what you do, who you serve, your unique selling point, and your call to action. As mentioned before, conduct A/B test campaigns and keep the ones that deliver the best.

3. Don't change too often, and be patient

Don't change your ad content or targeting every day as you need to leave enough time for the Google machine to serve your ads to your audience. Leave your ad untouched for at least three days before altering your ads. Remember, if Google gives £75 free credit, this should set the tone of the minimum amount you need to spend to achieve success.

Budget: ££

Complexity: Hire an expert

Time required: A few weeks for implementation

Strategy 48 – Promotional incentives

Promotional incentives are overused and often expected. Retail sales used to be twice a year to mark the end of a season, but now they seem to be almost every other month.

How to use them effectively, so you don't diminish your brand value perception and increase your cash flow?

- Don't do it too often.
- Offer different, exclusive promotional incentives for new prospects and VIP customers.
- Determine a promotional calendar aligned with key annual events (Valentine's Day, Mother's Day, Christmas, Black Friday). To grab your prospects' attention, you can start your promotional incentive before everyone else starts theirs.
- Announce your flash sales and time them to raise their fear of missing out (FOMO).
- Consider your launch close to payday to ensure they have money in their bank account.
- Create limited package offers.
- Offer a free gift with a purchase.

Budget: £

Complexity: Easy to moderate

Time required: Continuously

Strategy 49 – Retargeting ads

Do you have any idea how many people have visited your website today? Do you know who they are? If you don't, you are missing out on the opportunity to convert them into customers. Most individuals don't make an immediate purchase when they visit a website for the first time, so it is your responsibility to bring them back to you with retargeting ads. Ninety-six per cent of your first-time visitors are not ready to purchase from your website right away. So, don't let them go.

To be able to do that, you need to have the right website technology such as web cookies or Facebook pixel if you are utilising social media advertising. Retargeting ads is essential to target your first-time visitors through other marketing channels and encourage them to return to your website.

Naturally, it will increase your prospect engagement, thus making your entire campaign cheaper and more cost-effective.

Strategies to keep customers coming back:

- Install cookies and Facebook pixel plugin on your website.
- Retarget them with personal and customised content.
- Offer them some incentives, so they make an immediate purchase or request for more information or be contacted.
- Be creative to stand out.

Budget: ££££

Complexity: Agency required

Time required: It varies

Strategy 50 – Facebook ads

Do you know what is Facebook main goal? Facebook's goal is to keep users on the platform as much as possible. If your Facebook ad receives great engagement, your cost per click will reduce. This is why it is crucial to effectively target your audience, using demographic, interest, and location-based factors. As a result, you will be able to attract new customers and grow your turnover.

Tips for creating a Facebook ad:

- **Know your audience before you start targeting them:** an ideal way to do this is by creating a customer avatar of the ideal customer. Create at least 3 avatars for you're A/B test.

- **Create lookalike audiences:** Facebook allows you to use a tool that helps find customers who are similar to the ones that you currently have, making the campaign more efficient. This is why Facebook pixel is crucial as it will identify users similar (lookalike audience) to your website visitors.

- **Focus on mobile content:** Like most people that use Facebook currently, use it on a mobile yourself; it's imperative for you to focus more on mobile-friendly content rather than desktop. Mobile content will always work on a desktop, but not vice versa.

Tip: Target your competitor audience to maximise conversion.

Budget: £ to ££££

Complexity: Do it yourself or work with an expert

Time required: Continuously

Strategy 51 – Instagram ads

Instagram has more than one billion active users and therefore, the potential to help you reach your dream customers. To succeed, target the right audience by doing A/B testing, and the results will be unbelievable. Research shows that Instagram ads are perceived as non-intrusive, meaning that people will not be annoyed if they see your ads even though they don't follow your account. Since there is a greater interest in them, you have a higher potential to convert leads into sales. Furthermore, Instagram ads are favourable to everyone since the cost of the ads is quite low compared to traditional advertising.

How to attract customers using Instagram:

- **Work on your copy first**

Grab your audience's attention with an unusual statement or question to start with, for example, "Let me tell you why dieting will make you fat." It is unexpected and intriguing, and naturally, you will want to watch what the rest of the content is about. When creating your content, speak less about you, make your customer the hero of the story and tell your audience what's in for them.

- **Work on your visuals**

The more creative the visuals of your ads are, the easier to increase engagement.

- **Use videos to increase engagement**

Videos have, on average, a higher conversion rate so lose your shyness and smile at the camera. You can also use video from your customers. If you already studied with my branding and marketing programme, use those mind hacks in your Instagram ad.

Budget: £ to ££££

Complexity: Do it yourself or work with an expert

Time required: Continuously

Strategy 52 - Podcast ads

In 2020, there were over 1,500,000 active podcasts and over 34 million podcast episodes. We are in the area of the growth of on-demand audio. Podcasts are up 157% since 2014 thanks to the internet of things (IoT) and the growth of smart speakers and connected cars. Millions of people around the world are listening to podcasts every day, and this number is not going down. So, do you think you can reach out to your prospects via the world of podcasts which are streaming on YouTube, Apple Podcasts, Spotify, and other platforms? The answer is yes.

Podcast advertising is currently worth almost £700 million globally. Companies and entrepreneurs are advertising on podcasts because it works. Podcasters produce content for a very specific audience; in my case, my podcast *Tech Brains Talk* Podcasts are for marketers, entrepreneurs, and CEOs in the world of tech. Anyone interested in reaching out to this specific target audience will likely have a successful conversation rate. The advertising is unlikely to decrease, but to grow.

Why podcast ads are effective:

- Podcast ads are native, and the ads integrate seamlessly into a podcast episode.
- Listeners are active listeners, so they will listen to podcast ads.
- Listeners have a loyal relationship with their favourite hosts.
- Listeners do buy products or services suggested in a podcast ad.

How to attract customers through podcast advertising:

1. Identify the podcasts that target your dream customers.

2. First attempt, request to be a guest on the podcast by providing three topics the podcast host will find of value to his listeners.

3. Make sure your approach is always personalised. I know, as I get bombarded with requests to be on the Tech Brains Talk podcast,

and I only respond to the ones who took the time to do their research.

4. If the first approach doesn't work, ask to set up a meeting to discuss advertising on their podcast.

5. For effectiveness, I would suggest advertising for three episodes minimum to get the most exposure and traction. Remember, your prospects aren't likely to buy on the first interaction, so don't quit too soon.

Budget: £ to ££££

Complexity: Easy to moderate

Time required: It varies

Strategy 53 - Twitter ads

Twitter ads are probably the least popular social ad strategy among small business owners, while still being a very effective one. Twitter provides a number of great interactive tools that you can use to make your Twitter ad campaigns more engaging:

- Create a contest and combine with your own hashtag to maximise reach.

- Capitalise on big events, for example, is there a world cup championship that you can align your brand with? Find a way to win awareness by aligning your products or services to big national or international events.

- Use your customers and share stories people can relate to.

- Know your client persona and segment effectively using the demographic and psychometric tool provided. You will be surprised by the number of details Twitter ad tool provides.

- Video, video, video always performs better. Use one of those video editing phone apps to make a short montage with photos if you don't have a limited budget.

- Offer a free guide and add a call to action button on your visual to grab attention.

How to attract customers using Twitter advertising

1. Set your goals, then use Twitter's campaign types to help drive results around one metric. This is important, as it will define the content you need to create, the metric to measure, and action(s) you will pay for.

2. Set your campaign objectives. With each Twitter campaign type, you can only focus on one specific objective. If you want to drive traffic to your website, you should run a website clicks campaign.

3. Scale your Twitter campaign. When you have achieved successful results in one campaign, don't stop there. Scale it to achieve bigger

results. You can do this by layering multiple, successful Twitter campaigns to scale your results.

Budget: £ to ££

Complexity: Easy to moderate

Time required: Continuously

Strategy 54 – TV ads

Fewer consumers watch TV as more are watching on demand. Nothing is stopping your brand from diversifying your TV ad campaign across other channels. For a successful TV ad campaign, it is about being memorable and engaging your viewers to take action.

How can you achieve that?

- Tell them who you are: Present your brand or product clearly.

- Be a creative storyteller: Tell a story with emotions in the most unexpected way.

- Tell them what to do: Ask your viewer to take action at the end of your commercial.

Budget: ££££

Complexity: Agency required

Time required: It varies

Strategy 55 – Amazon

Oh, Amazon! Is it like marmite? You hate it or love it? Well, no matter how you feel, it is impossible to ignore; Amazon has a strategy to get customers. With millions of customers shopping on Amazon, your chance of finding your customers are pretty strong. Amazon has put in place services to support entrepreneurs starting out with a monthly selling plan package. The fulfilment by Amazon (FBA) does the storage, packing, shipping, international export, returns, and customer service for you. You also get the perk to offer free shipping for Amazon Prime members.

Your job is to make your products attractive by presenting them beautifully with a full description of the benefits. Then Amazon's algorithm lets potential customers discover you among a list of recommended products on their website. You can also utilise Amazon's large network of affiliates to help you sell your products by allowing them to feature Amazon ads on their own websites.

How to win customers using Amazon:

- This is an SEO game. Your products won't be discovered if they aren't properly optimised. You must include your brand name, product title, description with benefits, search terms used by your potential prospects, size, colour, etc. Don't go lightly with this task as it is crucial for your success. This is how customers will find you.

- This is a price and value game. Amazon shoppers are driven by price first and look to get the best value for their money. Do your research and see what your competitors are offering. Adjust your price-value proposition to increase your conversion. For example, if you sell zinc supplements for £11.99 and your competitors sell theirs for £10.99. Look at their product description and brand presentation to identify how to make your offer superior.

However, if you are not selling unique products, compete on price or add additional perks to increase your product value. E.g. Get this zinc supplement with a complimentary wealth guide written by our award-winning nutritionist.

- Be obsessed about customer reviews. Get as many customer reviews as possible as this is a crucial purchase influencer. This will leverage your advantage. Great reviews will attract more customers. After a few weeks or few days, reach out to your Amazon customers and ask them to give you a 5-star review.

- Always offer great customer service post-purchase to avoid unhappy customers writing bad reviews which will quickly have an impact on your conversion and sales.

Budget: £

Complexity: Easy to moderate

Time required: Continuously

Strategy 56 – eBay

You are, for sure, familiar with eBay. eBay is different from Amazon. Why should you sell on eBay? Well, eBay gives you a global reach with customers anywhere around the world. eBay was among the first tech companies to include gamification to encourage engagement with a product or service. How? The auction listing. If you have a bulk stock of products, you have the option to use the fixed price listing. However, if you have limited stock and demand is high, you will benefit from the auction listing. Let shoppers bid to buy your products. Like Amazon, eBay also solves the shipping problem of global sellers.

In comparison with other merchants, eBay charges lower fees for product listings but charges a final fee like a sales commission after the sale. To increase your sales, utilise eBay's affiliate programs by working with multiple affiliate marketers who will promote your products to receive their affiliate commission. So, if you have something unique that a lot of people want, eBay is a great place to start.

Budget: £

Complexity: Easy

Time required: Continuously

Strategy 57 – Amazon PPC

Amazon pay-per-click (PPC) is the equivalent of Google AdWords. You can appear on search results throughout Amazon by optimising product details for a search, but this may take a while. However, you can improve your customer acquisition effort by combining it with Amazon PPC. It is an advertising model for Amazon vendors where advertisers pay a fee to Amazon when a shopper clicks on their ad. The cost-per-click (CPC) will depend on the highest bidder. The difference between Amazon PPC and Google AdWords is that sales have a direct influence on a product's organic ranking on Amazon. Which means, the more sales that are generated via Amazon PPC ads, the greater the improvement in your organic ranking search.

How can you use Amazon PPC?

Sponsored Brands

Create Amazon ads to promote your brand. With this type of ad, you can promote your brand logo with a custom headline and up to three products. This also allows you to send shoppers to your custom Amazon landing page or your store page.

Sponsored Products

Create Amazon ads to promote individual products. This will appear when shoppers perform a product search at the top. Your product ads can also appear on external websites if you choose to use the sponsored products 'Extended Ad Network Beta.' You can retarget visitors who aren't browsing products on Amazon to allow them to view your product detail pages again, so they make a purchase.

Product Display Ads

Create Amazon ads to direct Amazon shoppers to your product detail pages. They usually appear below the "Add to Cart" button on Amazon product detail pages. Moreover, they can also appear at the bottom of the search results or on the right rail of search results.

Budget: £ to ££

Complexity: Easy to complex - Hire an expert

Time required: Continuously

Strategy 58 – Billboard

Billboard advertising is part of traditional marketing. Despite the passing of time, it is still around because it converts. How many drivers still drive and are stuck in traffic every day? It is effective, but unfortunately not affordable for many small businesses.

If you have the budget to pull out your own billboard campaign, here is a tip to get it right:

- You have a few seconds to grab their attention, so make sure your story/message is clear, short, and easy to understand.
- Go big or go home, so keep your text short and emphasise your visual as it should speak a thousand words.
- You have to grab their attention, so use contrast and colours.

Budget: ££££

Complexity: Agency required

Time required: It varies

Strategy 59 - LinkedIn prospecting

Getting a premium LinkedIn account is still by far the best investment I ever made for my business. With a monthly subscription fee of around £60, it was a no brainer. I just needed to close one deal to make more money back on their annual subscription. Remember, investing means you value the importance of making a return. If your prospects are B2B customers, you know the importance of connecting with the people behind the brands. Your ideal B2B customers are most likely to be on LinkedIn. No other B2B platforms compare to LinkedIn, so, create your account, revamp your profile, and upgrade your account.

In order to prospect on LinkedIn, the premium account gives you access to the sales navigator platform. With the sales navigator platform, you can:

- Conduct extensive prospect searches and access networks beyond your 1st and 2nd degrees of connection.
- Message people who aren't connected with you.
- Discover brand and industry news which allow you to personalise your prospect outreach.
- Create and save a prospecting list.

How to prospect effectively on LinkedIn:

1 - Have a killer profile presentation

We talked about it in strategy 34. If your LinkedIn profile reads like a sales page, people will be reluctant to speak with you. People buy people, so please make sure your LinkedIn profile is crafted to appeal to your target audience. Remove any irrelevant information and add relevant ones. If you worked at McDonald's when you were 16 years old, you might want to take this off.

2 - Join relevant groups to expand your 2nd degree of connection

Join groups where your prospects are likely to be. Group interactions on LinkedIn are probably one of the weaknesses of the platform. People don't really interact but share posts and hope for the best. Why should you join a group then? Because you will expand your 2nd degree of connection and increase the chances of being discovered by more people on LinkedIn.

A quick reminder on LinkedIn connection types:

- 1st degree of connection: people who are directly connected to you.

- 2nd degree of connection: people who are connected to your connections but not to you.

- 3rd degree of connection: people who aren't connected to you or your connections.

3 – Use hashtags

- Take the habit of adding three hashtags at the end of each post. Why? Your post might be featured by LinkedIn.

- Find your prospects by using hashtags. Create hashtag searches to find LinkedIn users posting about a particular subject. If your target audience is fintech companies, they are likely to use the hashtag #fintech when they post content. Click on the hashtag to identify all users posting about fintech. Connect with any users who may be a relevant to your customer acquisition.

4 - Apply my 10 x 5 LinkedIn outreach - be personal and consistent

Take the time to search for and filter your dream clients. Make ten personalised connections each day, five days a week. That's it! No more than that. You will achieve much better results and secure more meetings in no time. It is only effective if your approaches are tailored. Use your calendar to schedule your ten daily approaches. Do it as the first thing you need to do in the morning because the world will distract you if you leave it until later.

When it comes to bots on LinkedIn

If you decide to use external bots on LinkedIn, be very mindful:

- LinkedIn may block you and may close your account permanently as it is against their terms and conditions.

- We can smell a rat! Yes, we can sense that some LinkedIn approaches have been carried out through automation. If you are playing a numbers game and aren't trying to build long term relationships, then do what you believe is best for you.

Budget: 0 to £

Complexity: Easy

Time required: Continuously

Strategy 60 – Taxi advertising

When you operate in a saturated market, achieving the best results out of advertising efforts requires some creativity and doing things differently from your competition. That's where taxi advertising can help you stand out.

Fashion brands, beauty brands, entertainment brands, and tech brands are among the industries who have effectively tapped into this strategy. When the online fashion brand 'Pretty Little Thing' started their first taxi ad campaign in April 2017, it helped grow the brand, and they haven't stopped since then. Why? Taxi advertising provides a physical presence, increases brand credibility, and makes a tangible, physical impression on consumers.

Customised vehicles are not only for tradesmen, and a lot of businesses can tap into taxi advertising as an alternative. Vehicle wraps are eye-catching and also memorable. It's an excellent way to build brand awareness, reach a wider audience, and advertise in specific locations. Try this non-aggressive campaign for a local or national campaign and win new customers.

To do it effectively:

- Use bold colours or visuals to catch people's attention.
- Explain what you do or your unique selling point in one sentence.
- Add a call to action and/or your website details so your prospects can find you.

Budget: ££££

Complexity: Hire an expert

Time required: A few weeks for implementation

Strategy 61 – Let's spin the wheel

Have you heard of marketing gamification? Well, this is one of them, and at 3 Colours Rule agency, it is something we do a lot for our clients. If you are selling business to consumers, the spin wheel is your ultimate sales booster! It is designed to boost your sales by offering your visitors a chance to win discount coupons just by spinning a wheel on your website store.

The spin wheel is another plugin that can be added to your website and helps you convert your visitors into customers by adding a "wheel of fortune" to your site. This marketing tool can help you grow your mailing list, transform visitors into instant customers, and increase sales by offering discounts.

The reason why the spin wheel plugin is so effective is that it integrates FOMO marketing, the fear of missing out. The discounts are timed, therefore if your visitors are really interested in buying from you, they are likely to buy instantly so not to miss out your offer.

Budget: 0 to £

Complexity: Easy

Time required: Less than an hour

Strategy 62 - Handwritten sales letter

How many emails have you received since this morning? I bet its too many, and at least half of them will be deleted without being opened. It becomes harder and harder to get the attention of your dream customers through so much noise.

This strategy is effective if your business doesn't require a large volume of customers to be profitable. If, for example, your business needs to secure 10-50 high-quality clients per year to be profitable, the handwritten sales letter could be an effective customer acquisition strategy for you.

Why is a handwritten sales letter so effective?

- It allows you to get through the gatekeeper.

- It has a 100% open rate. You will always open a letter with your name and postal address handwritten on it, won't you?

- It is personal and makes the receiver feel special.

How to write successful handwritten letters to get customers:

1. Make a list of your 15 dream clients and do your research. Your sales letter should feel personal, so the recipient notices that you have done your research on them. Please stay professional; I'm talking about business here.

2. Use beautiful stationery; remember this is your brand. You should write your letter on branded stationery paper. You are taking the time to write this sales letter, so make the best brand impression.

3. Write your letter by hand and keep it short and structured. Your letter should have a clear introduction about you and your business, a paragraph or two that breaks down your pitch, and then a conclusion with a call-to-action for your prospect.

4. Wait a few days and follow up with a phone call as your prospect will be more receptive. It's your duty to engage well to convert as many prospects as possible.

Budget: 0 to ££

Complexity: Do yourself or hire an expert

Time required: Continuously

Strategy 63 – Deal websites

Ok, don't roll your eyes with this one. This is not only for dropshipping businesses. Have you bought a service or a product from a deal website like Groupon? Most likely, yes. The reason why those deal websites are still there is because they are effective for many businesses. The reason why a business would be prepared to offer deals on these websites, despite the fact that it will reduce their profit margins, is to get a customer into their sales funnel. If you have low brand recognition, low client retention, or need a cash flow boost, this could work for your business. However, most companies using deal websites aren't doing it effectively.

How to achieve the most success when using deal websites:

Once your customer enters your sales funnel by purchasing one of your products or services, it is your opportunity to build loyalty and upsell. Your goal is to get them to upgrade their offer after product or service delivery or get them to repeat their order. Basically, view these deal websites as part of your brand awareness strategy. This is your chance to offer a great brand experience to move your brand perception from commodity to brand delight. Customers that aren't familiar with you can become loyal customers and even brand advocates.

A few additional guidance points when selling your products or services on deal websites:

1. Do your due diligence. Make sure your website is compliant, so deal websites accept your offer applications. Calculate your margins to ensure you are still profitable after the third-party website fee, advertising costs, shipping costs, etc.

2. If you are planning to use different deal websites, please track your activity from the start by setting different offers or different discount codes for different deal websites so you can evaluate which deal website gives you the best conversion.

3. Create limited and timed offers to create urgency and boost cash flow. Renew your offers weekly to evaluate which deals create the most interest.

4. Promote your offers via your network. Your existing customers and followers may also be interested.

5. Dropshipping companies love deal websites, but to compete well against them position your products or services to appear more affordable to your customers.

Budget: £ to ££

Complexity: Easy

Time required: Continuously

Strategy 64 - Birthdays

The reason we stay loyal to some brands and not to others is because of how they make us feel. The brands that make us feel special and exceed our expectations always win. So, do you know your audience's birthdays? This is relevant wherever you serve B2B or B2C clients. If you don't know your customer's birthday, it is time to ask.

Are birthday messages effective? Birthday emails have:

- 500% higher transaction rate than promotional emails.
- 350% higher revenue per email than promotional emails.
- 200% higher unique click rates than promotional emails.

We buy on emotions, and when our birthday occurs, rationality will fly out of the window. Any unjustifiable behaviour is justified by "It's my birthday, after all. I can get what I want"

Phase 1 - How to delight your existing customers:

Send birthday cards (virtual as an option) with:

- Birthday coupon.
- Limited special discount.
- A gift to your most loyal customers.

Phase 2 - Strategy to get new customers

Use your existing customers to attract new customers. When providing a birthday gift or special offer to your existing customer, invite them to share the experience with someone else. This allows them to introduce a new potential customer with an interest in your products or services.

Phase 3 - Plan it and repeat

See your customer reach grow every year with this exponential growth hack strategy

Budget: 0 to £

Complexity: Easy

Time required: Continuously

Strategy 65 - Charity

Consumers are looking more and more for brands that go beyond. Brands who seek to make an impact within their industry. Are you one of them? Being a great brand is no longer sufficient. What brands do to support society's issues will drive consumer choices. What your brand does to give back to your community may not reflect instantly on your sales KPIs, but will impact on your consumers' unconscious decision processes. So today, having a corporate social responsibility agenda within your company is essential. Societal issues multiply, and we all need to contribute to resolving them through philanthropy, activism, volunteering, or donating to a charity.

You may be raising your eyebrow, wondering what this has to do with attracting customers or how partnering with a charity will help you get customers. So, let me explain. Charities attract a number of wealthy philanthropists and companies seeking to give back to communities. When you choose to support a charity, this also allows you to give back to the community and expand business opportunities. Because of the nature of their donors, charities are well connected and have access to a large network of wealthy, influential individuals. Supporting a charity gives you access to relevant networking opportunities. Do you see the bigger picture now? Your network is your net worth.

How to connect effectively with a charity to attract customers while supporting a community:

1. Set your social responsibility agenda. What are the pressing issues within your industry? What needs to be done to resolve those? For example, if you were a toothpaste company, plastic waste and environmental issues should be on top of your social responsibility agenda.

2. Evaluate what your company needs to do internally. For example, should you create biodegradable toothpaste tubes?

3. Identify a list of charities that align with your corporate social responsibility agenda. Arrange meetings with those charities to identify the ones that fit best with your company culture and social responsibility agenda.

4. Define how you will work together and set your financial contribution. There are many ways to work with charities: events, donations, free products or services, etc.

5. Communicate with your network about your involvement with a charity to raise your brand likeability.

6. Ensure the charities communicate about your brand so you can build your brand awareness through their network.

7. When the relationship is established, arrange for them to connect you with other donors to open new business opportunities.

Budget: £ to £££

Complexity: Easy

Time required: Continuously

Strategy 66 - Flyers & catalogues

I have to say it again. The most common mistake I see businesses make is to wait for customers to find them. It sounds so obvious, but many businesses underestimate the importance of combining outbound marketing activities with inbound marketing activities. You need to include outreach activities to get to your customers. Printed material falls under the outbound category. I repeat, having a beautiful website, a strong LinkedIn or Instagram page, and even physical space, it will not necessarily be enough to get customers to come to you. You need to let them know you exist.

This strategy is ideal for local and online businesses. Flyers are still effective; let me show you how to do it the right way:

1. Decide what you want to achieve with your flyer campaign.

2. Create your copy which should be short and to the point: why you, why this, and why now?

3. Add a call to action and a reason to act now.

4. Use bold colours that are aligned with your brand guidelines.

If your business is new, use this strategy to announce the arrival of your business and provide limited special offers.

Don't neglect your distribution strategy:

- Mailbox.
- Coffee shops.
- Community centre.
- Co-working space.
- Events.
- Goodie bags but avoid if there are already too many flyers in the bag.

Budget: £ to ££

Complexity: Hire a graphic designer

Time required: Continuously

Strategy 67 – Merchandising

Oh, merchandising, so often misused and, however, so effective. Merchandising products such as branded pens, mugs, power chargers etc. are often used during exhibitions to grab people's attention. The only thing it is doing is attracting freebie seekers, and that's not the goal.

Branded merchandise should be used for more than driving traffic and only attracting potential customers' attention. Merchandising has a number of different marketing benefits. If your market is saturated, it is a great way to stand out from your competition.

Use branded merchandise to:

- Grab attention quickly and build awareness. In this scenario, it is not about conversion but brand awareness only.

- Build an emotional connection with your brand. For example, if your customers are likely to have children, create branded teddy bears with your brand on it. The kids will play with it, the parents will be delighted, and your brand is constantly in front of them. Likelihood of remembering your brand and choosing your brand when the moment is right is strong.

- Customer acquisition and engagement. Insurance companies have been using branded merchandise to effectively attract customers for a long time. Create a highly desirable branded merchandise that customers can get for free when they purchase your product or service.

Budget: £ to £££

Complexity: Hire experts

Time required: Continuously

Strategy 68 – Cold calling

Cold calling is not dead. It is still effective if your outreach is targeted, and your offer is desirable. Back in the day, picking up a phone book and dialling a random would have worked, but now, times have changed. Cold calling can be a numbers game, and you have to know this number, so you don't get discouraged after twenty calls.

How to get customers from cold calling:

1. Start with identifying your ideal customers and create a targeted list of prospects.

2. First, send a cold call email that gets their attention. Use tracking tools to identify if the emails have been opened. Your prospect will either respond, forward, or delete your email. Remember to always do an A/B test.

3. If your prospect is interested in finding out more, you should arrange a time for a phone call.

4. Now that your prospect is more receptive and more attentive to your business get on the phone.

With this cold calling strategy, your job is to ensure your lead is warm before you pick up the phone, then use a great script to close the deal. Over to you.

Budget: £ to ££

Complexity: Do it yourself and hire a sales expert

Time required: Continuously

Strategy 69 - Sales funnel

You have heard the term sales funnel before but really what does it actually mean? The sales funnel is the customer acquisition journey you create to transform a stranger into a customer who buys one or multiple products or services from your business. As you create brand awareness, many people will show up, but as their journey continues towards making a purchase, some of them will drop out.

Most companies, when building their sales funnel, focus on getting a customer to buy one product. If someone is interested in buying from you, why not suggest more products or services relevant to them? You should consider an upsell and down-sell strategy.

Vistaprint company is great at optimising their funnel. Vistaprint is an online printing service designed to help small businesses and entrepreneurs design and print branded and marketing materials. If you have ever used Vistaprint, then you will know how smooth they are. If you haven't, please try out of curiosity and for business research purposes. You may intend to order just a hundred business cards, but by the time you get to the checkout, you have placed a thousand business cards in your basket because they were only £5 more expensive, and also 20 mugs for £15, and headed paper because it was such a great offer. That's called a multiple upsell offer.

How to build a great sales funnel:

1. Think about your target audience(s). What can you offer them to get them through your sales funnel fast? At this stage, your aim is to build brand trust or instant gratification. You can do this in various ways:

   a. Free tool to use

   b. Ebooks or whitepaper

   c. Newsletter sign up

   d. A voucher or discount code

e. Free training.

2. Now, think about your products and/or services and figure out how they link together to align with your customers' goals and personal agenda. Remember, Vistaprint understand that if their customers need business cards, they are likely to need more than business cards when networking and prospecting. Think about it the same way. It is your responsibility to think about your products or services as solutions to support your clients' goals. If you are Nike and your clients buy running trainers, suggest socks and leggings to support their fitness activities. I usually suggest not more than one or two upsell offers to avoid annoying your customers. You can also create offer bundles that your potential customers cannot resist.

3. Track and adjust your funnels until you are happy with your conversion rate. Again, A/B test your funnels. If you have an online store, you can use algorithms or plugins to create upsell and down-sell offers. If you are selling a limited number of products, such as a one-course programme, work on your email copy to build trust.

Optimised funnels will:

- Create awareness and build leads
- Provide detailed insights about your prospects' behaviour to then increase conversion
- Save you time and reduce human errors through automation
- Increase sales.

Budget: 0 to ££

Complexity: Hire an expert

Time required: Continuously

Strategy 70 – Affiliate programme

Affiliate programmes are great if you do not have a sales force. They have helped entrepreneurs and business owners make millions. Not only do they continue to achieve a great return on investment for business owners, but also it is one of the cheapest customer acquisition strategies you can apply today.

Who can be part of your affiliate programme? Your existing customers and anyone who believes in your business offerings and can sell on your behalf. In return, they will get a commission for any purchases made as a result of their referrals. This strategy allows anyone to grow their revenues without breaking the bank.

How to make affiliate marketing work for you:

- Set up your own affiliate programme, or it's easier to join an affiliate programme website. This is ideal if you have an eCommerce business.

- Find affiliates who will be interested in promoting your products to their network. This works with social influencers and your customers alike.

- To get more affiliates to reach out to you, add an affiliate link to your website.

- Don't wait for them to come to you, recruit them. For you to increase your success with an affiliate programme, make sure your brand looks professional and desirable.

- Build strong relationships with your affiliates, so they know how to best promote your products or services, and so they can provide insights to improve your offerings so you can innovate.

Budget: 0 to £

Complexity: Easy to moderate

Time required: Continuously

Strategy 71 – Loyalty program

Did you know that having a loyalty programme can increase your customer retention by 5%? A loyalty programme reduces the cost of customer retention and consequently increases your profit. I know what you are thinking; this is great for B2C businesses not for B2B, but you couldn't be more wrong. I'm surprised that many B2B businesses have not yet tapped into this opportunity.

A loyalty programme is an excellent way to thank customers for choosing you. Everyone loves to feel appreciated. With technology now at your fingertips, you can set up, in minutes, your own loyalty programme with loyalty websites. It is not as complicated as it sounds. Be more than a collection of points, that's boring. Make sure your customers see the prizes available to them to improve their customer engagement. Make your loyalty programme a great engagement and brand experience tool. Think beyond the points to the actual rewards your customers will value and appreciate.

Budget: 0 to ££

Complexity: Easy to moderate

Time required: Continuously

Strategy 72 – Referral marketing

Most people spend time with people who are similar to them. What is stopping you from starting a refer a friend programme? It will cost nothing but an initial time investment and will increase your sales and profit exponentially. Why do you believe social influencers have such an influence on many people? 90% of people trust brand recommendations from their friends, family, social influencers, and other customers. You could tell the world how great you are, but it will never have the same impact as if your prospects hear those words from someone they trust. It is time to actively transform your existing customers into brand advocates.

A referral marketing strategy to attract customers:

- First, you obviously need to offer great products and/or services and great customer service. If you aren't great at what you do, forget this strategy, as you might spread bad publicity for your brand.

- You need to have a great incentive in place for both the referrer and the referee. Referral programmes usually use money as an incentive, but it is often not effective because everyone offers the same. I would recommend choosing a tangible product or service and change the incentive offer regularly. We have a short attention span and will skip anything already seen or expected. So, don't offer predictable incentives.

- Create referrer levels. The more they recommend you, the more benefits they can get until they reach the VIP level!

- Have fun with it.

Budget: 0 to ££

Complexity: Easy to moderate

Time required: Continuously

Strategy 73 - Employees

Brand trust in the eye of the consumer is harder and harder to achieve. However, content spread by employees remains a reliable trust factor for your prospects. Employees' trust, especially in B2B businesses, is crucial as you need to serve fewer customers. Are you actively engaging your employees as your brand advocates or simply don't know how?

Because prospects and customers view your employees as individuals who know the truth about your brand and as the ones who are likely to be honest about your products and services, you should amplify their voices to increase prospect conversion.

How to use your employees brand voice to attract customers:

1. Your employees should know your brand vision and mission, which means what you are trying to accomplish as a business, and what needs to be done to get there. When they understand that, articulate why they matter to your business and the role they can play in achieving this vision. If you don't treat your employees fairly, it is very unlikely for them to become your brand advocates.

2. Work on your brand culture. How do you want everyone to treat each other through words and actions? Create activities to allow employees to bond with one another.

3. Acknowledge their efforts both internally and externally so they can feel valued.

4. Invite your employees to use their platform to talk about your brand. Employees talking about your brand shouldn't be done from your brand social pages as it will lose the impact you seek.

5. Reward them through customer engagement and experience. You can have your own system or use websites such as Perkbox.

Budget: 0 to ££
Complexity: Easy to moderate
Time required: Continuously

Strategy 74 – Sales representative

The temptation to delegate your sales activities to someone else is so strong when you have the budget. In strategy 1, I talked about the importance of improving your sales skills so you can develop your own winning sales process that generates customers on a regular basis. So, before you jump in and hire a sales representative, generate enough sales to give yourself some financial peace of mind. In your conversion cycle, you should evaluate how much you need to invest before seeing a return on investment.

How to attract customers using a sales representative:

- Good sales representatives will have no issue accepting a low basic salary with a great commission. Hire someone who is confident and hungry to succeed.

- If you choose to hire someone with more robust expertise and insights about your industry, ensure they have an existing network of connections to tap in to.

- Hire people with experience in your industry and across several others, so they have developed adaptability, flexibility, and a broad knowledge base.

- Hire a consultant before you make them an employee as it will reduce your overheads costs, time, and stress. When you are ready to hire a full salesperson, have a sales training manual ready, so they can be effective from day one.

Budget: 0 to £££

Complexity: Moderate

Time required: Continuously

Strategy 75 - Growth hacking

Growth hacking; don't worry, it is not illegal, but it is by far one of my favourite customer acquisition strategies. What is growth hacking? It's the use of a variety of marketing tactics that work systematically to keep attracting consumers and grow exponentially. Uber and Dropbox both combined creative thinking, technology, and social media to achieve their growth. If you have used one of these brands, remember how you came to know about them. Maybe you were recommended, then you recommended to others and were rewarded for any successful customer acquired thanks to your help. Dropbox grew from 100k to four million customers in just over a year, which, in the end, cost them very little. This is growth hacking. It costs almost nothing and requires no extra time as long as you have the right marketing technology in place.

How to do growth hacking effectively to attract customers:

- Start with great ads to attract your first customers.

- Don't focus on a single tactic, but rather on multiple ones to increase your growth exponentially.

- Make it easy to sign up and for them to recommend you with social media sign up integration, so they don't waste time entering their details multiple times.

- Use marketing technology to automate referrals, registration, and the allocation of rewards for referrals.

Budget: £ to ££

Complexity: Easy to moderate

Time required: Continuously

Strategy 76 – Door to door sales

When I finished university, I struggled to find a job as I had three degrees, no experience, and a French accent that was too strong, according to some recruiters. I wasn't in despair, so I looked for a job that could pay my rent until I could find my dream job. I worked as a translator, and I was bad at it. I worked at Debenhams as a lingerie expert, don't ask me what I saw. Then, I found myself doing door to door sales. I don't recall how I found this job offer, but everything about this experience was new to me. It was one of the most challenging jobs while also being the most rewarding. It was a 100% commission. Some days I would meet amazing individuals, and others the most bizarre people. I lasted two weeks because of the great British weather. Despite the excellent commissions, I wasn't cut out to handle the rain, the cold, and the extremely long hours. You are probably wondering why I listed this strategy when I did such a bad job convincing you to do it.

Well, door to door is by far the least popular strategy, but the overhead cost is low, there is no ad blocker unless they choose not to open the door, there is no competition, and if you hire a great salesperson with a great personality, you increase brand likeability.

It's challenging but effective if you do it right:

- Know which areas to target. Different neighbourhoods will have different classes. It's important to identify the lower, middle, or upper class and how to communicate effectively with each one. When I was prospecting in council flats, I had to be more direct, but when I was prospecting in residential areas, I had to be more suggestive in my sales approach.

- Dress the part and prepare your pitch. If you waffle at the door, it will affect your confidence and brand trust.

- Understand the importance of body language. In face to face interaction, it is always about body language and tone of voice. Use your facial expressions, arms, and voice to accentuate important information. Remember the way you sell to the lower, middle, or upper class will be very different.

- Selling is not a numbers game but the more doors you knock on, the closer you will get to your next customer. So, don't give up and have fun.

Budget: £ to ££

Complexity: Easy to moderate

Time required: Continuously

Strategy 77 - Retail distribution

If you are selling tangible products but don't see the value in, or don't have the budget for, opening your own store, retail distribution is an excellent strategy for customer acquisition. With the expansion of e-shopping, loads of consumers are buying online, but nothing can beat a great brand experience that you can only get in-store.

How to get started with retail distribution:

- Do your research. If you want your products to be on the shelves of the most prestigious retail spaces such as Harrods, Galleries Lafayette, or even Sainsbury's, identify their requirements. Don't get disheartened if you don't fit all the requirements; you can still apply if you believe you have something, they would love to offer their customers.

- Find a distributor specialist who has the contacts and expertise to get you in front of retailers. This is where branding is important, as the competition is very tight.

- Be financially prepared. Calculate how much margin you are ready to let go for brand awareness and customer acquisition. Keep in mind the payment terms of retailers are usually three months after a purchase is made.

Budget: £ to ££

Complexity: Moderate to complex

Time required: Continuously

Strategy 78 – Brand ambassadors

The ongoing battle to turn customers into loyal brand fans is continuous. With a very fickle audience, you need to find new ways to keep them engaged while supporting their aspiration and achieving your vision. For this customer acquisition strategy to work, you need to identify your most loyal customers. By focusing your marketing activities on them, you have the opportunity to drive more customers towards your brand.

How to use your brand ambassadors to acquire new customers:

- Set your business goals.
- Pick a selected number of loyal customers for your brand ambassador campaign.
- Make them the centre of your next campaign by promoting their relationship with your brand, while making them the hero.
- Allow your brand ambassadors to express their creativity.
- Create exclusive activities for your most loyal customers.

Budget: £ to ££

Complexity: Moderate to complex

Time required: Continuously

Strategy 79 - Partnership

A partnership is another great and effective strategy for customer acquisition and brand innovation. Partnering with a brand that compliments your offerings makes products or services more appealing. Complementary brands will never compete with one another but instead, complement one another.

How to make your next partnership a successful customer acquisition:

- Which complementary companies serve the same target audience as you and will benefit from working with your business? Identify five businesses from five categories; do your research and make a list.

- Now you have your list, do your brainstorming. Evaluate how to present your brand to them to be perceived as a valuable potential partner for them.

- Agree on the terms of your collaboration in advance to avoid making any assumptions, such as partner promotion strategy, a communication plan to promote each other, commission etc.

- Measure, review, adjust, and repeat if you are successful.

Budget: 0 to £££

Complexity: Easy to moderate

Time required: Continuously

Strategy 80 - Joint venture

Joint ventures and partnerships may sound similar, but they are different. A partnership focuses mainly on cross-promotion of each other's service, but, with a joint venture, each business will dive a bit deeper. In a joint venture, you use your expertise and knowledge to create a new product or service that will appeal to each other's audience. So, you usually start with a partnership before moving to the joint venture stage. For example, H&M, the fashion brand, works with a number of top fashion designers to create special fashion collections. It is a great way for haute couture designers to be discovered by H&M customers, and for H&M to innovate and attract new customers themselves.

In a joint venture, sometimes both brands can access each other's client lists, prospect databases, and even marketing resources. Joint ventures save you time and optimise resources needed to attract new customers.

If you have just launched your business, it may be difficult to attract the right joint venture partners as you need to prove yourself, since established companies won't benefit as much from a joint venture with your new business because of your lower level of resources.

When your brand is established, you will benefit in various ways such as increase in enquiries and sales, brand exposure and credibility, customer acquisition growth, website traffic through backlinks, optimisation, and social media engagement.

Budget: £ to £££

Complexity: Moderate to complex

Time required: Continuously

Strategy 81 - Business ecosystem

The ultimate brand success is an ecosystem that continuously attracts customers. But first, what is a business ecosystem? A business ecosystem is composed of customers, influencers, associations, partners, and other relevant and interested parties that unite to collaborate and deliver astonishing products and/or services to advance their industry and improve their competitive advantage. It is easier to create when your brand is established and has credibility unless disruptive innovation is at the heart of your business.

How you can use a business ecosystem as a strategy to acquire customers:

1. Evaluate the weakness of the market and identify the partners that seek to improve their competitive advantage to grow their market share. Key questions to consider are: What is the market need? Who can help you achieve your vision? What can your business do for them?

2. When you have selected the brands part of your ecosystem, expand your business focus on the vision of the collective and consider one to two business strategies and a six-month plan.

3. Measure, review, adjust, and repeat if you are successful.

It is essential for your business to really know your customers to form your ecosystem strategy. The best approach remains to broaden your customer challenges from a holistic perspective and then choose the right partners to include in your ecosystem.

Budget: £ to ££

Complexity: Complex

Time required: Continuously

Strategy 82 – Coworking spaces

If your business is located within a co-working space, well, hello customers! The rise of co-working spaces has transformed the way we work. More start-ups and established businesses love this modern business environment. Co-working spaces, perceived as "cool", are great to attract not only customers but also employees who are looking for a modern work culture.

If your services or products are tailored for entrepreneurs, start-ups, or freelancers, you just hit the jackpot. Seeing a piece of cake every day, at some point, you will want it. *You* are the cake by the way if you didn't get the analogy.

How to attract customers through co-working spaces:

- Arrange a meeting with the co-working coordinator to ensure you are aware of all the opportunities available to you.
- Brand your office exterior, so people walking by know what you do.
- Offer special, complimentary services to other tenants.
- Get featured in the newsletter through an interview combined with a great limited offer.
- Join the online directory.
- Attend networking events.
- Offer free workshops and present your products and services.
- Get out of the office and speak to people in the coffee break area.
- Speak to the co-working space manager so he/she can introduce you to other tenants or coordinate collaborations.

Budget: 0 to £

Complexity: Easy

Time required: Continuously

Strategy 83 – Product placement

Have you watched Transformers 4? No? Did you notice that 55 brands, yes, 55 brands were plugged in the movie? From Budweiser to Armani to Yili milk? If you have no idea what product placement is, let me explain. Product placement is a subtle, and sometimes not so subtle, placement of brand products within a movie, TV show, music video, or other performances.

Why is it effective? It is native, doesn't disrupt, and is effective for brand positive association. If you think about James Bond, all men want to be James Bond. The car he drives, the suits he wears, the watch on his wrist, and the women he… well, you know. These are positive and brand associations which will unconsciously impact on consumer choices. Getting a superhero to drink Pepsi will have a direct impact on sales.

This strategy is not the cheapest, but if you have the budget, the impact will be continuous while the movie or music video is a success.

Budget: ££ to ££££

Complexity: Complex

Time required: Continuous

Strategy 84 – Trade industry entities and chambers of commerce

Joining trade industries and chambers of commerce offer many benefits that will boost your business:

- Being a member of trade industry entities solidifies your business position within a niche market. You improve your credibility and, therefore, favourability. According to The Schapiro Group, B2B consumers are 80% more likely to purchase goods or services from your brand if you are a member of a trade industry.

- You will increase your brand exposure through their promotional activities conducted for your brand. This usually includes their website, social media, community events, newsletter print advertising, and magazine.

- You also have the power to raise your brand voice by playing an active role within the trade industry entities and chambers, which is great to access local government and media coverage.

- Utilise all networking opportunities to meet other members who may become potential customers or referrers. Take the opportunity to speak when the opportunity arises so you can be heard by everyone. Naturally, people will come to you if you offer something they are interested in.

- Sponsor events to take the opportunity to present your business to an attentive audience.

Budget: £ to ££

Complexity: Easy

Time required: Continuously

Strategy 85 - Mobile games

Digital ads are everywhere, and now, consumers barely engage with them as they used to. It has become obvious that it has become challenging to engage consumers through social media. It is important to be creative and innovate to engage consumers nowadays. To get your consumers' attention, you have to educate, inspire, motivate, and entertain.

More and more people are playing games. Some gamers spend over five hours per week on mobile games. A surprising fact; the average serious female gamer is 38. Why are mobile games so popular? It's a great way to kill time during a commute or when you don't want to speak to someone annoying. Mobile games, as some people believe, are not only for boys. Do you remember Pokémon GO? All ages, backgrounds, and genders were hooked on it.

How to get customers through mobile gaming:

1. Advertising. Classic and straightforward.

2. Brand placement. Imagine your logo appearing in The Grand Theft Auto game? Ok, I chose the most controversial game, but you see my point.

3. Run a competition prize. This is a great way for the mobile gaming app to engage its users to play, and for you to increase brand awareness and engagement.

4. Create your own game. What is stopping you from creating your own version of candy crush? Don't start from scratch; instead, collaborate with a mobile gaming app and change some features to promote your brand.

Budget: ££ to ££££

Complexity: Complex

Time required: Continuously

Strategy 86 – Community

As mentioned above, more and more consumers will choose brands that go beyond the delivery of their service or products by doing more to support the community. What have you done for your community lately? Sing that question like a Janet Jackson song until you get the song reference. Participating in community activities allows you to help while promoting your brand, products, or services to a local or specific community.

How to attract customers through community engagement:

1. Identify communities where you are likely to find your customers. Choose three and narrow it down to one as this will take a lot of your time.

2. Participate in community activities and events.

3. Wear branded clothes and be prepared to help. If you have the opportunity to sell your products or services, even better. Make a good impression to be remembered and attract regular customers for your brand.

4. Secure an interview on their website to improve your SEO.

5. Communities crave great stories to share. It won't be as difficult as getting an interview with the BBC, I can guarantee it. Before your interview goes live, make sure to provide your business name, address, phone number, social media accounts, and website.

Budget: 0 to ££

Complexity: Easy

Time required: Continuously

Strategy 87 – Events

Have you run your own events before? Well, yes, well done. If not, what are you waiting for? There are many benefits to running your own events. I know what you are thinking; I have no budget or time or energy to start this. Well now, with technology, you really only need a laptop, internet, social media, and an event booking website to get going. Yes, you can start that simply and upgrade when your company is ready to splash that cash to impress the masses. Organising your own events is a great strategy to raise brand awareness, bring prospects to you, and even attract sponsors.

How to run virtual or live events successfully to attract customers:

- **Set your goals**

You could put up an event to grow your customer base, drive sales revenue, educate customers, and recruit new employees, inviting potential customers so you can present and demonstrate your services or products. If your business is innovative, your prospects will be sceptical about being the first to purchase from you. Putting on events allows them to discover without pressure and build a personal relationship at the same time.

- **Your customers**

Invite your existing customers to speak on your behalf. It will be your credibility in front of your prospects while making them feel appreciated for being loyal customers to your brand.

- **Logistic**

Establish your budget, find your venue, and select your team and tech to ensure the event runs smoothly.

- **What's unique about your event?**

How can you get the attention of your dream guests? How can you get them excited to attend? Could it be a well-known guest, a celebrity, free food and cocktails, or something else? When you figure out how to get people to attend your event, the rest becomes a piece of cake.

- **Do your marketing and cross-promote**

Engage with the right channels, which means the channel where you'll be able to reach out to your ideal event guests. If you have speakers, invite them to promote the event through their network. This should be a mix of social media, email campaign, adverts, word of mouth, content marketing etc.

During the event is where you can make all your dreams a reality. Sorry, I'm being dramatic:

- Be a dream host, and leave no room for surprises. Arrive early enough to ensure your venue is ready and is dressed and ready to your standard.

- Introduce yourself to your guests and invite them to interact by introducing them to one another. Your duty is to make sure everyone is having a great time, and no one is alone, talking to a bowl of French fries.

- Invite your guests to share event photos on social media as this will allow you to create some buzz during and after your event. You should suggest an event hashtag when posting about it on their social media. Invite them to share photos and videos from the event. Remind your guests throughout the event to post on social media with your hashtag. Include a prize draw to engage them to participate.

- Capture the moment. If there is no proof, it will be like it never happened. Put someone in your team in charge of taking photos throughout the event so you can use them for the upcoming event promotion.

- Next day, thank your guests for coming and share photos and videos about the event to create some envy.

Budget: 0 to £££

Complexity: Easy to complex

Time required: Continuously

Strategy 88 – Exhibitions

Trade shows played an important part in the global success of the luxury tea brand, Pukka. Sebastian Pole and Tim Westwell, the founders, sold the business to Unilever for an undisclosed sum. So yes, trade shows and exhibitions work. You don't have to hunt for your customer; they will come to you as little red riding hood came to the wolf.

They are not only an excellent source of new leads but also a powerful way to grow your brand awareness within a specific industry. Most businesses don't choose this strategy as a first option as the upfront investment is quite high with the possibility of no return. But the reason why some businesses don't achieve their goals or make a return with this strategy is that they don't apply the right approach.

Having a stand or booth is not enough. Your main goal is to attract the highest number of visitors to your stand so you can evaluate if they are the right prospect or are just after the goodies on offer. Connect with the serious ones and convert them into warm leads or even customers.

Strategies to attract customers at trade shows and exhibitions:

- Check the list of exhibitors. Other exhibitors may be potential customers or partners with whom you can collaborate through the trade shows. For my first exhibition, I secured a partnership with Suzuki. They brought traffic to my stand, and I brought traffic to theirs. It's an excellent strategy, not often used by exhibitors.

- When you have your list of potential customers or partners, contact the event organisers and ask them to coordinate an introduction. You should do this not less than six weeks before the start of the show because, at this point, they won't have time, or it will be too late to coordinate a meeting to discuss opportunities.

- The way you present your stand is everything, so don't neglect your presentation as it will impact on the value perception of your brand. Most often less is more, but make sure it is clearly branded.

- Be a creative attractor; don't be too entertaining or too serious as you won't attract anyone to your stand, or the wrong people just looking to be entertained. Find creative ways to offer a taste of what you do so you can attract potential customers.

- Be welcoming. Yes, your body language and your position within your stand is everything. Don't sit behind your desk or at your table all day with your eyes on your laptop or phone waiting for people to come to you. Stand up, smile, make eye contact when visitors walk by.

- Be wary with giveaways. Use them to attract visitors but position them inside your stand, so you get a chance to speak to them without them nicking all your chocolates while you are looking the other way. It will naturally differentiate people who are serious from the goodie hunters.

- Be all over social media. Let people know in advance you are exhibiting, invite your prospects to meet you, and carry on communicating throughout the event.

Budget: ££ to £££

Complexity: Complex

Time required: Continuously

Strategy 89 – Event sponsorship

Can't organise your own event? Well, event sponsorship might be a perfect solution for your business and an effective way to raise your brand awareness. Let someone else bring your ideal customers to you in exchange for a financial contribution. Event sponsorships are great to help you achieve your business goals, as they increase brand awareness and credibility. The reason why they are not perceived negatively is that they are not intrusive or a pushy advertising approach.

On top of commercial events, you can also get involved in social cause events. These build your positive brand perception as you get the opportunity to attach your business to worthy causes.

How to get the most of event sponsorship:

- Sponsor the right event, so do your research. Do the event organisers have a track record of delivering great events? Do your due diligence and leave no room for guessing games. Speak to previous sponsors and check out if they have repeat sponsors as this is a good sign.

- If you have a limited budget, start with a small event, or stay local until your marketing budget expands. You can find many local events on event or trade show website listings

- Create content and use social media to let the world know you are a sponsor. Use your complimentary passes to invite potential customers.

Budget: ££ to £££

Complexity: Complex

Time required: Continuously

Strategy 90 - Sports events

Most companies conduct marketing and sales activities during working hours, but you are not like everyone, and that's why you are reading this book. Your prospects are more than their job. They have a life after work, and you can be involved in that, too. You have clear prospect personas for your target audience, which should also include their extracurricular activities. Is it golf, dance, tennis, swimming, or something else?

By sponsoring or getting involved in sports events, your brand naturally promotes a healthy lifestyle. It's also a great strategy for your employees to connect outside of work with your potential prospects. This is where bonds are really created. When choosing an event, think about the brand association you want to create.

How to win customers with sports events:

- **Brand association for distinction**: Get your brand name attached to a sporting event, so you develop a natural and favourable brand recognition when exposed to competition.

- **Employee satisfaction**: Attract and retain your team by sponsoring events where they can participate. Naturally, they will spread the word through social media which exponentially expands your brand reach to your next employee or customer.

- **Sponsorship hospitality**: Allow sports personalities to meet with potential customers. It is a great way to open a dialogue with a prospect while delighting them. You could sponsor a football player worthy of recognition and aligned with your brand.

Budget: ££ to £££

Complexity: Easy to moderate

Time required: Continuously

Strategy 91 – Annual celebrations

When people are in the mood to celebrate, they spend. So, annual celebrations are excellent occasions to create products or services for these celebrations, special offers, and further activities to engage and convert your prospects and customers.

Here are a few to start with:

- Valentine's Day
- Pancake Day
- Mother's Day
- Saint Patrick's Day
- April Fools' Day
- Easter
- Father's Day
- Pride
- Notting Hill Carnival
- Halloween
- Bonfire Night
- Remembrance Day
- Christmas & Boxing Day
- New Year's Eve

Budget: 0 to ££

Complexity: Easy to complex

Time required: Continuously

Strategy 92 – Conferences

Do I love conferences? Yes, I do. Why? Because it is an effective way to get insights from experts in your industry while expanding your network. Attending a few conferences every year is essential for your business. Surprisingly, a lot of people who attend conferences haven't managed to generate business opportunities yet. If the idea of attending a conference with thousands of strangers frightens you, worry no more, I have some suggestions for you here:

- Set your goals before you get there. Mindset is essential, so decide what you would like to achieve in advance. Find out if the list of attendees and speakers is available so you can best prepare yourself. How many meetings do you want to secure with potential prospects or partners? Who do you definitely want to speak to?

- Network like a pro. Be realistic, you won't have the chance to speak with everyone, so aim to have meaningful conversations. When entering a networking room, always walk to a group of three. Why? There will always be two listeners and one talker, so it is easier to break the trio into two duos and rebalance things out.

- Don't take more than ten business cards. Don't give your business cards to everyone. Keep your business cards for prospects or potential partners. Connect with others on LinkedIn using the QR code. This way, when you go back to the office, home, or your hotel, you know you only have people's cards with whom you may want to do business.

- During the talk, always take the microphone and ask a question. Why? This is the perfect chance to grab everyone's attention by saying who you are and what you do and asking a very good question so everyone can see how clever you are. People will be naturally drawn to you during the networking after the session is over because you have become visible.

- Dress to impress and be distinctive. Women can easily wear a colourful dress or suit. For men, wear a nice red tie or another bright garment so you can be easily distinguished from the crowd.

- Reach out to speakers and organisers as they might open up new opportunities. If you want to be on stage next year, this is a perfect opportunity to grab their attention, but don't do it when they are running around.

- After the event, follow up with the prospects and potential partners within 24 hours maximum to arrange a meeting if you didn't get the chance to do it during the event.

- After the event, apply what you have learned. The conference was great, but if you don't apply the insights you received during the conference, what is the point? So, review your notes, discuss with your team and set a plan to apply what you learnt to make your company even more appealing.

Budget: 0 to ££

Complexity: Easy

Time required: Continuously

Strategy 93 – Book

I have to admit, writing this book was a challenge because I don't see myself as a writer, and along the way, I managed to find all the possible ways to procrastinate to avoid doing the thing I needed to do the most; write this book for you. I'm extremely glad I didn't give up. I know this book will be among my proudest achievements, and I can't wait for you to share your stories with me. I want to know this book had an impact on your business and on your life.

If you decide to take on the challenge to write your book too, it will come with a lot more advantages. A book gives you authority and credibility and solidifies your expertise. It also raises your brand visibility and, consequently, gets you the attention of the media.

A book gets you closer to your next customers and gets people talking about you. When you get that attention, you should redirect it to your products or services. A book integrates smoothly into your sales funnel. You bring in prospects through a low-ticket product, your book. Naturally, they will start following you. Use that attention to sell the next product in your funnel and continue upselling until they reach the premium products. Does this feel like an "Aha!" moment? I hope so! Now, go and write your book.

Strategies to make your book work for you:

To sell your consulting services, online training, or coaching services

- To secure speaking gigs
- To launch your mastermind
- To sell tangible products
- To sell a tech product or services (e.g. software product)
- To promote a 'done for you' service.

Budget: 0 to ££
Complexity: Easy
Time required: Continuously

Strategy 94 – Webinar

Have you ever bought a product or service after watching a webinar? Quite likely, it has happened. You may think webinars are overrated but don't be fooled; webinars are effective. To make your webinar into a money machine, you have to delight your prospects by providing amazing, valuable content before they commit to anything. Naturally, if you hook them with great value and they can see you as the key to achieving their dreams, you will have a new customer. So, start running webinars to attract large numbers of leads to the top of your funnel, and close the deal.

How to run great webinars that attract customers:

- Pick a niche you want to target. The more specific your niche, the more conversion you will get at the end of your campaign. Instead of targeting business owners, choose fintech entrepreneurs.

- Run an ad campaign to get your specific niche to register to your event. Pick a great hook for your webinar title. Your webinar should clearly state:

  o Who it is for.

  o What they will learn and what they will be able to achieve.

  o Why they should attend.

- Prepare amazing content. If your content is average, your webinar attendees will drop out throughout your live webinar, and you want to avoid that because humans are copycats. When one does something, others often follow.

- Prepare an unlimited offer that is only available for webinar guests. Your offer must be hard to resist and must have a time limit. Such as "Get the offer before we end this webinar," or, "Offer only valid for the next 12 hours." For products or services below £2,000, prospects are usually prepared to take the offer on the spot.

    o   Offer a lot of guarantees to remove scarcity (e.g. refund if unhappy)

    o   Share client testimonials to reassure them.

My webinar success story

One of my first businesses was my online fashion styling academy, which, by the way, still exists. After ending my career as a fashion consultant, I decided to transform my knowledge into an intellectual property that would serve other aspiring fashion stylists. I spent two years creating my four courses, and now I was ready to sell. I ran a Facebook campaign at the end of December as I knew most people look for a new career in January. I had over a hundred sign-ups across two weeks with a daily budget of £5. My webinar was called, "How to start a fashion stylist career even if you have no budget or no experience in fashion." The hook was set. Through the delivery of my webinar, I provided great insights and made them a great offer. I generated £5,000 in one-and-a-half-hours. I remember jumping with joy as I couldn't believe how much money I had made in such a short amount of time during my 1st webinar.

A few more presentation tips:

- Practice like crazy. Why? It will reduce your anxiety if you are not comfortable talking in front of a lot of people.
- Make you sure you have a great microphone.
- Tell stories because they keep your audience engaged.
- Keep asking questions to your audience to keep them engaged.
- Use stories, facts, and examples to support your idea and strategy.
- Be friendly; people buy people.

Budget: 0 to £
Complexity: Easy
Time required: Continuously

Strategy 95 - Speaking

I was told once that public speaking was among the top biggest human fears. Do you want to be a thought leader in your industry? Well, you will need to start speaking so you can get there. Being confident speaking in front of an audience allows you to demonstrate your expertise, gain great credibility, engage with target audiences, and create raving fans. Sounds great, right? Are you ready to speak then? Please don't say no. You've got this. Start small before you hit the big stage. Let me put it this way; when you go to a conference, it is impossible to speak to everyone, but being on stage puts everyone's attention on you. The level of trust you create in the mind of your prospects is unmatchable.

How to use speaking engagements to drive leads for your business:

- Pick your expertise. Choose what you want to be known for. As a keynote public speaker, my expertise is in marketing psychology and creativity. I chose this because I'm a creative who loves psychology and marketing. Surprisingly, not a lot of people are familiar with neuromarketing, which is great for me. My style is 'edutainment.' I want my audience to have fun while learning with me. Visit 3 Colours Rule YouTube to watch my talks.

- Your appearance is key, but your presentation is too. Less text and more visuals are always better.

- Conclude with a call to action. The aim is not to sell on stage, but for them to contact you, so you add them to your sales funnel.

Budget: 0

Complexity: Easy

Time required: Continuously

Strategy 96 - Mentorship

If there is one thing I wish I'd known sooner, it's the importance of having the right mentor. No matter how far you are along with your career, everyone should have someone to whom they can go for advice. Entrepreneurs with mentors are more committed, achieve better results faster, and often become great leaders. You might think, well this is great, but what does it have to do with getting customers? Everything!

- A great mentor is someone who is where you want to be. They have achieved business success and will share all they have learned with you so you can achieve the same success sooner, and even greater.

- Having a great mentor will open the door to his or her network. Your network is your net worth. Tap on all the opportunities your mentor can give you.

How to get a mentor?

- Your mentor can be a stranger. I started getting mentored by reading the autobiographies of all the successful entrepreneurs, listening to their podcasts daily and following them on social media. You are the average of the people you spend the most time with. Choose your entourage wisely.

- Another strategy I used to get a mentor was the free lunch interview. I would invite my dream mentor for a lunch interview at a nice location. I made sure my interview request was appealing by articulating the value for them to meet me. After a few encounters, when I felt we connected, I would ask them if they would be interested in mentoring me. The answer was always yes.

- A lot of successful entrepreneurs become mentors. They often charge. This is the last option if the strategies above aren't sufficient.

Budget: 0

Complexity: Easy

Time required: Continuously

Strategy 97 – Pre-launch prospect building campaign

Have you heard of *The 4-hour Workweek* book by Tim Ferriss? If you haven't, I would suggest reading it after this one. No matter the type of business you have, this book will stimulate your creativity, as this is what happened to me. I was fascinated by his business model. Working only four hours per week? How did he do that? He had put in place an efficient process run by a team who had various degrees of responsibility which automatically freed up his time to do less and be richer.

After reading this book, I was inspired, and I decided to launch a fashion business concept for fun. I wanted to test out what I had learned from this book. To minimise failure, I did a pre-launch campaign to test if there was enough interest in this brand. This is a strategy 3 Colours Rule agency carries out often with our business clients to avoid wasting unnecessary revenue for the launch of a new product, concept or business. The brand was mini me & moi, a T-shirt brand for mothers and their children. The concept was pretty simple, matching t-shirts for mothers and their child, made on purchase order received. We created a landing page, and my graphic designers did the artwork. Then, I only needed to advertise. I focused on Facebook to reach out to my audience.

Why a pre-launch campaign attracts customers:

- It allows you to validate your business concept interest before you start spending loads of money. Are there enough people interested in buying what my business offers?

- It allows you to build your list of potential customers. Keep posting to stimulate their desire, and when you are ready to launch your products or services, they should sell like hotcakes.

- It allows building your brand credibility in front of investors if you have no track record as a new business.

So, what happened with my launch? I created one creative campaign to highlight with humour the beauty and comedy of being a mother. I specifically targeted prospects who followed my competitors: Mothercare, Childsplay, and many other luxury brands for kids. The result? In two weeks, we had over 1,500 submitted email addresses of prospects and over 6,000 engaged Facebook followers. I achieved this with a daily budget of £5. Why was it so cheap to run? The Facebook algorithm favours ads that perform well. The more popular your ad is, the cheaper each click becomes. Each click cost 0.02, which made my budget last longer.

Budget: £ to ££

Complexity: Easy to Complex

Time required: Continuously

Strategy 98 – Private clubs

When you think about private clubs, what comes to your mind? Fat old men smoking cigars deciding on the fate of the world? Ok, maybe it's only me who has watched too many conspiracy movies. The gentlemen's club used to be and still is, a private social club originally set up by men from Britain's upper classes in the 18th century. Those clubs were associated with the British Empire until it was replicated across India, Pakistan, Bangladesh, and America. They allowed men to discuss business affairs in a social setting where they had access to a bar, a library, dining room, and so much more. Over the years, the perception of gentlemen's clubs was negative, and they started to allow more women in. However, call me paranoid; I do believe secret gentlemen's clubs still exist.

Today, being more gender-inclusive, private clubs have become an ideal place to meet high profile individuals. The requirements to access a private club require an evaluation, recommendation, and a substantial annual membership fee. All these hurdles to gain access to these clubs make them even more desirable. While in the club, your networking skills come into play so you can connect with potential partners, influencers, and, of course, customers.

How to choose a private club:

- Identify what type of members are part of this club as you want to make some meaningful connections.
- Evaluate the perks, facilities and networking opportunities so you can benefit exponentially and make a return on your investment.
- Identify your frequency allowance so you can evaluate how often you can use the facilities by yourself and with guests.

Budget: £ to ££

Complexity: Easy to Complex

Time required: Continuously

Strategy 99 – Table for six

Last, but not least, is my own customer acquisition strategy creation, and I'm delighted to share this one with you. Have you been part of a network of managing directors, business owners, or businesses operating in the same industry and didn't get as much out as the effort you put in? You attended events, participated in the regular group meetings, introduced your network to contacts, and even had one-to-one meetings. There is nothing wrong with that, but a couple of years ago, I realised that I could create a better economy of opportunities with six individuals. The table for six was born.

Why six? I was inspired by the six degrees of separation; the idea that all people are six, or fewer, social connections away from each other, globally. Consequently, we don't need a chain of more than six individuals to connect with relevant customers or other stakeholders. Through my table for six, I created a close network of individuals who don't compete but complete each other as we all operate in the same industry and serve the same type of customers.

How to create your table for 6:

1. Identify five individuals who serve the same target audience as you.

2. Choose individuals who are active networkers. If they don't regularly meet people, they won't be able to bring new opportunities to the table.

3. It is your responsibility to ensure the five individuals you bring to your table will get along. So, organise the first meeting to introduce everyone to each other and explain the concept.

4. Choose people who can commit to meet once a month. To allow them to plan their schedule, schedule all the events well in advance to ensure they keep the dates free.

5. When the table of 6 is set, meet once a month, and each of you should share one goal you are trying to achieve and the support you seek. As the leader, ask each individual to be as specific as possible.

6. Before the next meeting starts, each member presents the outcomes of the introductions made from the interactions and actions of the people at the table.

7. Repeat this every month. You can choose to include a mutual agreement where there is also a commission for successful introductions made.

Budget: 0

Complexity: Easy

Time required: Continuously

BONUS STRATEGY
THRIVING THROUGH A RECESSION

How have some businesses successfully navigated through a crisis or an economic recession? Although fear is healthy, panic is deadly for a business. History repeats itself, and some business tactics and marketing strategies have proven to have helped some businesses thrive through the recession and flourish afterwards.

1 - Understand your target audience's crisis behaviour

When things go haywire, act smart. In a crisis, it is a mistake to target and spend your marketing budget on a broader audience. Instead, you will earn your spurs by adapting leaner and efficient marketing methods. In good times one can categorise their target audience on the basis of standard rules of the book, such as demographics and psychometrics. However, in a crisis situation, it's more about understanding the emotional reaction of your target audience towards the economic environment.

2 - Don't arbitrarily cut your marketing budget, instead adjust it

It's understood that due to declined sales and less profitability during a crisis, companies tend to adjust their budgets. A common mistake is for businesses to dramatically cut their marketing budget. You should see marketing as an opportunity or as a crucial investment for the future of your company. It's the time when companies need to formalise better positioning and a more efficient messaging strategy to boost sales in the long run by placing themselves ahead of the competition during a crisis.

There are two basic things you can do:

- Maintain your media presence: Invest in a communication strategy. If your competitors are not cutting down on marketing, you will require enormous efforts to maintain your brand's voice and market presence in the longer run. I cannot stress enough, prevent damage by considering marketing as an investment.

- Bring more negotiating power: Negotiation is critical in surviving a crisis. What can you negotiate to enhance your marketing investments? What needs to be re-negotiated right now? You can possibly leverage less expensive PR to spread awareness for your brand, which can give a higher ROI in the longer run.

Invest your time to learn about the other side, for example, the situation, time limits, and willingness to compromise. If you are hit by the crisis, so are they!

3 - Rethink your product or service delivery to offer what your clients value the most

During a short-term crisis, it's important to be proactive rather than taking a leap of faith or holding back. It's the time when you should ask yourself, is there a better way to serve your customers or stop doing what is not essential and focus on the things your clients/customers really value?

A few key points to focus on:

- Communicate empathically to understand what your client/customers priorities are.

- Convey your strength, so they feel empowered to do business with you.

- Understand how the perceived value of your service/product has changed during a crisis, and then adjust your value proposition.

Likewise, build long-term customer trust in the values of your company, not only in your product.

4 - Focus on existing customers and turn them into your brand advocates

Studies from Harvard Business Review suggest that during a crisis, companies that managed to amplify their brand voice by maintaining or expanding their advertising and marketing spending were more likely to gain the market share in comparison to their competitors.

The three critical phases for your brand's success:

- Phase I - Emotion is the key ingredient that drives our thoughts, actions, and decisions. During a crisis, it's obvious that people are going through rapid emotional fluctuations from buying excessive toilet paper to accumulating groceries. Consumers are making decisions on the basis of anxiety and uncertainty. This is the moment to reinforce an emotional connection with your brand and demonstrate empathy.

- Phase II - This phase demands you showcase your actions. It should demonstrate that you value your customers by taking action, not merely by just saying that you stand with them. Instead, come up with the ideas that showcase that you're on your customer's side.

- Phase III - At this stage, you have to ensure that your customers still perceive the positive value of your product and buy from you. For example, for businesses, affiliations with charities and other aid organisations fighting against the crisis can influence purchasing decisions. This can potentially create more brand awareness and advocates for your brand.

5 - Increase digital marketing activities - test, tweak, and repeat!

In a crisis, digital marketing is more likely to give you results. Divert and invest your time in digital marketing. Brainstorm to come up with creative methods through which you can attract and mark your brand impression on the audience. At this time, when almost everything is locked down, and people are mostly leveraging social media channels, it's time to push on and create valuable content. The keywords here are "create value."

Online marketing can provide you with useful insights about your customer segment by giving you better measurability and trackability than ever before. As we say, numbers don't lie. It's the right time to collect data.

For example, it would be a smart idea to re-target the audience and spend your budget on those who visited your website, instead of running a campaign targeting a broad segment. Influencing the behaviour of someone who showed interest in your product is way cheaper than those who are not interested during the crisis.

6 - Improve affordability

After analysing the target audience and consumption categories in point 1, it's important to support your audience by empathising with them. My advice is don't disrupt your brand positioning. For example, if you are a luxury brand, don't cut costs drastically and diminish your value.

How to make sure entry is quick as much as possible:

- Reduce long term contracts.
- Make sure to emphasise the quality of your services/products.
- Offer flexibility by giving instalment options.
- If you are a Software as a Service (SaaS) company, you can possibly focus on giving a few features for free to generate awareness and brand credibility. This phase ensures that they still believe in your product, and they will still buy from you when things start to get back to normal.

7 - Have a pipeline of innovations ready to launch quickly when the economy improves

During a crisis, it's not just about managing budgets effectively; there is more to it. Consider using the ample time available to re-assess strategies and business practices by raising the right questions. Such as, is there really a need to bombard your audience with more digital ads, webinars, or newsletters? Does this really leave an impact on your consumer psychology? Or does this worsen the touchpoints which your brand had delivered in the past?

For this, you need to bring innovation into your marketing mix. If you ask me, it's more about scrounging your business objectives and brainstorming as a team. You need to analyse how you can fill the gaps when the economy improves.

Use a crisis as a pedestal to rejuvenate your marketing pipeline; give your pipeline some air to breathe. Analyse your past results; consider where you lacked and need more structure. Brainstorm; are there any channels you can eliminate from your marketing strategy and still achieve results from other initiatives?

A few questions you may ask yourself are:

- What have our customers complained about in the past?
- A deeper analysis of competitors and areas/markets they conquered?
- What do our customers wish we had? How can we deliver more value?
- Are there any new technologies that can enhance our marketing performance?
- What would the new future look like, and how can we adapt or fill a gap in the new market?
- Embrace the challenges and, hopefully, you will get useful results to innovate your marketing pipeline.

8 - Stay flexible; adjust your strategies and tactics

Success is when preparation meets opportunity. Under crisis, choosing the right mechanism for growth is crucial. Common ways for inorganic growth could be joint ventures (JV's), mergers and acquisitions (M&A), and strategic partnerships. Yes, it's a daunting task, but past results have validated this strategy. Partnerships are like a marriage. You want to make sure your partner is happy; otherwise, it won't last long.

According to PwC, before jumping for something like this, it's critical to understand:

- Capabilities: Filling a gap or building on strengths.
- Control: Weighing investment, access, and ownership.
- Cost: Determining the business ROI.
- Conditions beyond a company's control: Predicting success based on external factors.
- Keeping the right pieces: The role of divestitures in growth decisions.
- Best of both worlds: When a partnership and M&A make sense.

9 - Analyse and track everything

To keep you and your crisis business strategy on track, it's necessary to analyse and tweak your marketing measures on hand. It's inevitable not to maintain KPI. During a crisis, social listening will pay rewards for your brand reputation and business growth.

- KPI for analysing the impact of your strategy.
- KPI to measure the audience sentiments after implementation of the strategy.
- KPI to measure your online mentions.
- Correlation metrics to measure the numbers before and after PR activity.
- Brand mentions of social media accounts and hashtags.
- Maintain a log of audience feedback to better understand the key areas you can hit in the crisis.

10 - Be open to a new business model

When going through a rough period, don't forget to adapt. Adaptability is key. Businesses either fail or end up losing big when they become resistant to change. Identifying sustainable paths to grow your market share will deliver benefits for your firm. Before making any changes, try to analyse the situation from an open-minded perspective and ask a few questions before finalising things:

- Are there any parts of your current business model that won't work? Why? What can you do about it?

- Test your new business model assumptions so that they can fit your crisis sales strategy.

- Collect evidence to show your innovation will sustain after the crisis is over.

- Identify what limits the new business model when things start getting normal.

- Nevertheless, it's also important to analyse your internal capabilities before bringing any change in your business model. What else will be needed to provide a complete solution that supports the implementation of the innovation? It's just not about the crisis and temporary solution; it's about the long game.

11 – Stay positive; nothing lasts forever, your attitude is key

Your attitude will decide your company's altitude. It's not the first time we have all faced a crisis; we are all in this together. Feed your mind with positive thoughts and pump up your body with regular exercise, even if you are at home. Follow a daily routine to commit yourself to the goals you want to achieve for your company's success. Lastly, spend time with family and friends to ease your mental stress.

SECTION 7:

The work starts here

The end in mind customer acquisition plan

Congrats on reading the 99 strategies to get customers and my bonus on thriving for a recession, but now the fun really begins! Apply my 'end in mind' customer acquisition plan.

1 - Set your revenue goals for the next 90 days

- What revenue do you want to generate in after 90 days?
- How many customers do you need to get to achieve your 90-day revenue target?
- How many prospects do you need to reach to convert them into customers? If your average prospect conversion is 1 out of 3 prospects becomes a customer, multiply your prospect reach by 3.

2 – Set your customer acquisition budget

Most often, the reason why people fail to get customers is that they don't allocate enough budget for prospecting activities. Allocate 3-10% of that budget on marketing: the larger your turnover, the smaller your ratio. The average advertising spending for a business in a steady-state situation is between 5% to 8% of turnover.

3 - Think like a billionaire; what can you delegate?

- Which strategies are relevant for your customer acquisition approach? Write them all down and then conduct a process of elimination until they fit your marketing budget. Some strategies don't require any financial investment except for time, so don't cross them out if they are essential.
- Value your time and delegate tasks that can be done better and faster by experts. Delegate any tasks that are not related to your expertise or are below the value of your time. Hire a virtual PA to start with.

Think like a millionaire or billionaire; hire the best people to help you reach your business goals with as little friction as possible. When choosing experts, hire people with an amazing track record, so the risk becomes an investment. If you had to do it all yourself, it would take you years to learn all the expertise you need to scale in the next couple of years. You can't afford to lose time.

4 - Track like your life depends on it

- Set some KPIs to measure weekly
- Review them regularly and continuously
- Work with consistency to get traction

5 - The customer acquisition and retention

The beyond marketing model is a model I also created to help businesses retain customers. The beyond marketing model consists of transforming fickle customers into loyal customers. This should be one of your priorities. To summarise, don't spend all your time on your customer acquisition strategy without having a great customer retention strategy.

- **Collect data from the beginning**

Use Google Analytics or Adobe Analytics for a deeper insight into your customers. Use these insights to improve the user experience.

- **Create prospect profiles and map customer journeys**

Understanding your customers' behaviours and their journey through your sales funnel will help you personalise your marketing messaging and target your prospects more effectively.

- **Offer great customer service**

You will keep your customers for life if you make them feel valued. Go above and beyond to always exceed their expectations.

Download a free copy of my DAC system to execute your 90 days customer acquisition plan, visit https://www.3coloursrule.co.uk/dac

THIS IS THE BEGINNING

You made it to the end but this is the beginning. I hope this book helps you feel optimistic about your ability to get more customers. Send me a picture of you with this book and let me know how this book impacted on you and the people around you. Now, this is your chance to move people and the world forward. You have what it takes, and I believe in you, but you have to do the work.

If you enjoyed reading this book, I would like to invite you to discover:

- 3 Colours Rule, my branding and marketing agency where we help businesses build their brand value, credibility, awareness and loyalty www.3coloursrule.com
- Flavilla's online branding and marketing programme, which is ideal for new entrepreneurs and marketers seeking to develop their branding and marketing skills to grow their brand exponentially. www.coaching.flavillafongang.com
- Tech Brains Talk podcast where I have amazing conversation with tech extraordinaire who share the strategies that led them to success and how they are changing the world.

Thank you

Flavilla Fongang

SECTION 8:

Marketing and sales terms from the book

Marketing and sales terms from the book

- **AI**: Artificial Intelligence

- **B2B**: Business to Business

- **B2C**: Business to Consumer

- **Web cookies:** HTTP cookies, or Internet cookies, are built specifically for Internet web browsers to track, personalise, and retain information about web users

- **CTA**: Call To Action

- **CRO**: Conversion Rate Optimisation

- **CRM:** Customer Relationship Management

- **Downsell**: The act of persuading a customer or prospect to buy something additional or less expensive

- **Dropshipping**: an online business that sells products to their buyers without ever actually stocking any items themselves

- **Evergreen content**: Content that is continually relevant for readers over a long period of time

- **FOMO:** Fear of missing out

- **Gamification**: The application of typical elements of game playing to encourage engagement with a product or service

- **Google Crawler**: A robot or spider used to automatically discover and scan websites

- **IoT:** Internet of Things are internet-connected objects that collect and transfer data over a wireless network without human intervention
- **Inbound marketing**: Activities designed to attract visitors and potential customers
- **KISS**: Keep It Simple & Straightforward
- **KPI:** Key Performance Indicator
- **Neuromarketing**: The science of consumer and purchasing behaviour
- **Outbound**: Activities designed to push a brand, product, or service onto prospects for lead generation or customer acquisition
- **WordPress plugin:** software that contains a group of functions
- **PPC**: Pay Per Click
- **PR**: Public Relations
- **Prospect persona**: A representation of the decision-maker(s) you are selling your products or services to
- **QR Code**: Stands for Quick Response; a piece of information from a transitory media that is quickly readable via using a smartphone
- **ROI**: Return on Investment

- **Sales funnel**: The journey your clients go through to purchase your product or services

- **SEO**: Search engine optimisation

- **Tagline**: Catchphrase or slogan

- **Upsell**: The act of persuading a customer or prospect to buy something additional or more expensive

SECTION 9:

Tech tools to support your customer acquisition activities

Tech tools to support your customer acquisition activities

- **Asana**: A platform to manage a team's work, projects, and tasks online
- **Active Campaign:** To run email automation and more
- **Blinkist**: To listen to nonfiction books condensed into short audio clips
- **Buzzsprout:** To host podcast episodes
- **Calendly**: To schedule virtual or face-to-face meetings
- **Canva:** To create designs if you don't have a graphic designer
- **Dropbox**: To upload, save, and share your files online
- **Eventbrite**: To create event registration for online and physical events
- **Facebook pixel:** An analytics tool to measure the effectiveness of your advertising by understanding the actions people take on your website
- **Fiverr:** To find freelancers with various expertise; gig can start at five dollars
- **FlipHTML5:** To transform your pdfs into e-magazines or e-books
- **Google drive:** To upload, save, and share your files online
- **Google Calendar:** An online calendar which integrates with tools such as Zoom, Calendly or Oncehub
- **Grammarly**: A plugin that corrects writing mistakes
- **Hubspot**: A marketing and sales CRM

- **Hotjar**: To discover how visitors are using your website
- **Keywords everywhere:** A browser add-on for Chrome & Firefox that shows search volume, CPC, and competition on multiple websites.
- **Lemlist**: To send cold-call emails
- **Learndash:** A plugin to integrate online courses to your website
- **Meistertask**: A platform to manage team's work, projects and tasks online
- **Oncehub**: To schedule virtual or face-to-face meetings
- **PeoplePerHour:** To find freelancers with various expertise
- **Perkbox**: An employee benefits scheme designed to reward employees for their hard work
- **Phantombuster**: To extract data and take action automatically on the web
- **Slack**: A channel-based messaging platform
- **Microsoft Teams**: To run video calls
- **Upwork**: To find freelancers with various expertise
- **Yoast:** SEO plugin to write better content that ranks
- **Zencastr**: To carry out podcast interviews
- **Zoom**: To run video calls

ABOUT FLAVILLA FONGANG

An award-winning businesswoman

Originally from Cameroon, she was born and raised in Paris. She moved to London in 2002 despite being unable to speak English. Within her first year in London, she obtained a BA in Economics & Law, a BA in Marketing & Communications. A year later, she obtained an MA in International Business with distinction.

Flavilla Fongang is an international and multilingual keynote speaker. She spoke at the largest marketing events such as Advertising Week, AdWorld, MozCon, HubSpot, DMWF, and many more. She is a neuroscience brand expert covering strategy, design, marketing and customer experience. She is the founder of 3 Colours Rule, an award-winning branding and marketing agency. Flavilla was awarded the "She's Mercedes" businesswoman award by Mercedes Benz. Flavilla is the chosen brand advisor for the BBC and provides regularly actionable brand strategy advice. Her award-winning agency has already received multiple awards. She created the D.A.C. system and The Beyond Marketing Approach which have helped numerous brands successfully grow their business.

She is also the founder of Tech London Advocates Black Women in Tech, one of the largest TLA groups. Computer Weekly named her the 5th most influential woman in technology in the UK. She hosts Tech Brains Talk podcast providing insights and advice to tech entrepreneurs and companies. She is an entrepreneurship expert with the Entrepreneurship Centre for Saïd Business School, University of Oxford. She is a branding course instructor for various organisations. Flavilla was a guest marketing and brand strategy lecturer at Goldsmiths University, she mentored at London Metropolitan University.

She belongs to the African diaspora and met, at The Palais de l'Elisée, the President of France, Mr Emmanuel Macron and the President of Ghana, Mr Nana Akufo-Addo to discuss business opportunities in Africa.

Her determination extends to helping her clients achieve their goals and they appreciate her positive attitude and fun personality.

Printed in Great Britain
by Amazon

37929569R00106